End Time Prophecy
Revealed

Richard L. Madison

INTERNATIONAL EVANGELIST RICHARD MADISON

All Bible scriptures are quoted from the King James Version of The Holy Bible.

ISBN Number: 978-0-578-04423-1
Publisher Record Number: 1508747

Library of Congress Catalog
number: 2010921290

Published by Operation Healing Ministry

Contact information:
Evangelist Richard Madison
PO Box 205
Oakman, Alabama 35579
205-622-5022
www.rickmadison.org

Table of Contents

Reference...IV

Acknowledgment V

Foreword: End Time Revelation......................VII

Ch. 1 The Spirit and the Word..............................11

Ch. 2 Signs of Jesus' Return..............................21

Ch. 3 Rapture or Tribulation Saints....................67

Ch. 4 Can Anyone Escape the Tribulation?........79

Ch. 5 Eight Raptures Beginning With Enoch.....85

Ch. 6 The New World Order............................107

Ch. 7 Seeing in the Spirit................................123

Ch. 8 Generations in the Bible........................131

Ch. 9 The Meaning of Jacob's Troubles...........141

Ch. 10 Nineteen Year Prophetic Cycles...........167

Ch. 11 The Covenant of Jerusalem...................173

Jerusalem Covenant Document..........................175

Prayer To Be Born Again...................................178

Ministry Products.............................179 - 185

About the Author...186

References

Kenneth Sharp, M.D. - Attending Trauma Physician, Vanderbilt University Medical Center
"Richard you are a living miracle. There must be a God in Heaven truly watching over you."

Mike Shreve, Evangelist and Publisher - Cleveland, TN
"I have known Rick Madison since 1987. The anointing of God is upon him to help people reach a new level of faith."

Pat Robertson - President, Founder, and Host of The 700 Club - Virginia Beach, VA
"Jesus walked into that hospital room, and laid His hand on Rick Madison's head and healed him completely."

Ron Weinbender - International Director of Full Gospel Businessmen's Fellowship International (FGBMFI) - Irvine, CA
"Richard Madison is truly an ambassador of the Lord in every respect. He is anointed to pray for the sick and share the love of Jesus."

Sid Roth - Founder of the Messianic Vision national radio program and It's Supernatural television show – Brunswick, GA
"Richard Madison was raised from the dead to preach and teach that Jesus is real and coming soon. Richard's book on healing is at another level."

Perry Stone – International Evangelist, Author, Founder and Host of Manna Fest TV Show -
"Rick Madison has one of the top three stories that I have ever heard in my life about people coming out of comas."

Acknowledgments

I would like to thank all the pastors who are so kind to allow me to preach the Word of God in their pulpits. It is an honor to work with you to win souls for the kingdom of God. Thank you for your friendship, prayers, and support to our ministry.

Special thanks to our dear friends, Rod and Susan, Chris and Brandee and Aunt Mary Lois. Many thanks also to Kevin, Martha, Sam, Alex and Duke for allowing us to stay in their home and finish this project. Thanks to everyone for all the ways you encourage us. Thank you for your awesome prayers, support and friendship.

Foreword by the Author

Receiving End Time Revelation

No one will ever know the day or hour of Jesus' Return. There are two reasons for this. First, there are twenty four time zones in the world. If someone said Jesus was coming at a certain hour of the day, it would not be consistent around the world. The second reason is because Jesus said so. God's Word will never change nor fail. Those that study ENDTIMES agree that we are in the last days. The Holy Spirit is revealing the mysteries of the Word to those that are hungry. The scriptures are opening for those that have an ear to hear. The prophecies of the last days become clearer as we study the scriptures. I hope to convince you that we are in the last days. I want to also prove that the scriptures reveal that there are eight raptures from Enoch to the white throne judgment.

A lot of people have never received a spiritual vision, dream, or even heard the voice of God. However, hidden manna is available for everyone that is hungry for intimacy and revelation from God. The Apostle Paul said we all see through a glass darkly. Many prophecies today are easy to understand because of world events unfolding. Everyone who studies the Word of God and prays fervently, can hear from God. The Lord has given man tremendous knowledge in the last 100 years, especially in medicine, science, and ways to travel. Daniel said knowledge would increase in the last days (Daniel 12:4). In 1986, I became very aware of the Holy Spirit after waking up out of a 27 day brain dead coma. I was pronounced dead on arrival after a head on car collision. I had several broken bones such as a broken neck, ribs, hip, foot and jaw. I had a ruptured spleen, torn aorta artery, punctured lung and I lost sight in my right eye.

During an out of body experience, Jesus came to me and put His hand on my head. He told me He was giving me another chance. I was to tell everyone that He is real and coming soon. I was told to preach the Word, pray for the sick, and signs and wonders would follow me. I woke up with full brain activity. I had received 400 staples, 9 surgeries, 3 steel plates, and 19 screws. 10 weeks later, I walked out of a wheelchair. Contact us for your copy of this faith building story titled **Raised from the Dead**. We also have a DVD with the reenactment of the story with actors. In July of 1986, God began revealing end time events to me through dreams and visions. It's difficult to explain all the prophetic events in just a few pages, so please read to the very end. Obviously, I can not cover every single prophecy in this book alone, but I will share a lot with you. Each chapter will explain more details of God's patterns and plans.

Here are some examples of the information that are in this book. In 1987, God spoke to me about two events that would occur in 1989. The Holy Spirit told me that one of these events would be a powerful earthquake occurring in California. The other event would be many thousands of Jews returning to Israel. In October of 1989, a powerful 6.9 earthquake hit San Francisco during the World Series baseball game. A month later, the Berlin Wall came down and over 250,000 Soviet Jews went home to Israel. In 1988, the Lord told me Iraq would soon cause a war, and the USA would be involved. This war would be over oil in Kuwait.

The United States went to war against Iraq in 1991. God said Israel would soon sign a seven year peace treaty. They did in 1993, but God said Israel would sign another seven year treaty in the future. This is symbolic to Jacob working two seven year periods to get the bride he intended on getting (Genesis 29:27). Joseph also interpreted Pharaoh's dream of two seven year cycles. Joseph said there would be seven years of harvest, then seven years of famine. We are in a time of harvest, but famine is on the way. On September 10, 2001, I was preaching in Tennessee and I heard the Lord say, "The world will change tomorrow and it will involve Middle Eastern people. Many will watch this tragic event on television." The next morning, terrorist highjacked planes and flew them into the

World Trade Center. The church had standing room only that next night. Everyone watched the news for days waiting for answers. Nine-eleven (9/11) will never be forgotten. In October 2007, God told me that the battle of Gog was very near. This is a war mainly between Israel, Iran, Syria, Lebanon, and Russia. Israel will win this battle and amaze the world. Israel will then sign a final seven year treaty with their Arab neighbors. This 2nd seven year treaty will begin the Tribulation period. Israel will build the third temple in Jerusalem and begin animal sacrifices for the first time since 70 A.D.

I will reveal the three battles of Gog mentioned in Ezekiel and Revelation. I will reveal why there are three views on the rapture (pre-trib, mid-trib, and post-trib) and why all three are right. I will also reveal the eight raptures in the Bible from Enoch to the White Throne Judgment. I will reveal the Two Witnesses, the next 9/11, and **when the next rapture may occur**. God recently revealed to me 12 different nineteen year prophetic cycles. These cycles occurred between 1900 and 2012. I will start out simple and then get deeper. It has taken me 25 years to learn, remember, and write down the information in this book. I can promise you that this book will take you to another level.

God bless you always,
Richard L. Madison

Chapter One

The Spirit and the Word

Jesus Christ is the true Word of God. The Word came down from heaven and took on flesh. He is the only Savior of the world. He is the only way to heaven. In Christ, we have joy, peace, truth, power and eternal life. Jesus manifests Himself to us by the Holy Spirit. People speak the oracles of God as the Spirit of God moves upon them.

The prophecy came not in old time by the will of man: but holy men of God spake as they were moved by the Holy Ghost. (2 Peter 1:21)

All scripture is given by inspiration of God, and is profitable for doctrine, and for reproof, for correction, for instruction in righteousness. (2 Timothy 3:16)

But as many as received Him, to them gave he power to become the sons of God, even to them that believe on his name. (John 1:12)

We that believe in Jesus Christ are born again, not by the will of man, but by the Holy Spirit. The Spirit of God will always agree with the Word of God. The Holy Spirit revealed the Word of God (Jesus Christ) to John the Baptist. John saw the

11

Spirit come down in the form of a dove and land upon Jesus. John declared Jesus as the Lamb of God, who would remove the sin of the world. Jesus had the Spirit of God without measure from that day. The Holy Spirit and the Word of God came back together and miracles began to happen.

And John bare record, saying, I saw the Spirit descending from heaven like a dove, and it abode upon him. (John 1:32)

And looking upon Jesus as he walked, he saith, Behold the Lamb of God. (John 1:36)

Revelation Knowledge

Peter also received revelation by the Holy Spirit when he declared Jesus as the Christ, the Son of the Living God. Jesus then told Peter that flesh and blood had not revealed this to him, but the Father which was in heaven. Jesus again told Peter that boldness and revelation is what the church would be built upon.

Upon this rock I will build my church. (Matthew 16:18)

He is a merciful God who will always love us with an everlasting love. He desires to give His people wisdom, knowledge, and revelation.

That the God of our Lord Jesus Christ, the Father of glory, may give unto you the spirit of wisdom, and revelation in the knowledge of Him. (Ephesians 1:17)

Paul suggested that we could all receive the same understanding that he had received, as we read the Word of God.

Whereby, when ye read, ye may understand my knowledge in the mystery of Christ. (Ephesians 3:4)

The Word of God is a mystery that is truly hid from the wise and prudent. We must be born again to understand or see the kingdom of God. We must be born of water and the spirit to enter into the kingdom of God. We thank God for the "logos" or written Word of God. We must also appreciate the Holy Spirit that brings life to the Word for our life and ministry. We are all called to be disciples.

Who also hath made us able ministers of the New Testament; not of the letter, but of the spirit: for the letter killeth, but the spirit giveth life. (2 Corinthians 3:6)

The Spirit of God gives us a "*rhema* word" or a living oracle of what is written. The Spirit of God will always reveal the Word of God. We must take every opportunity to read the Bible. This kind of effort allows our mind and spirit to be saturated with the Word. The Word of God should always be our foundation. The Spirit of God will never say anything contrary to the Word. We must know the Word of God in order to recognize what kind of spirit is speaking to us. When we hear a voice, we must compare it to the Word of God, to see if this is Jesus, the devil, or our own thoughts. Jesus said His sheep would know His voice, and they would not follow another (John 10:3-5). His sheep know the Word and await His voice. The Holy Spirit will also manifest Jesus to us. We believe in Him, even though we can't see Him.

Even the Spirit of Truth; whom the world cannot receive, because it seeth Him not, neither Knoweth Him. (John 14:17)

The Next Great Shaking

Sometimes end time prophecy and future events can only be understood as it unfolds before our eyes. The Holy Spirit speaks to us and then shows us where that prophecy is in the Word of God. We study to show ourselves approved. Pray for God to give you direction to help others know what time it is. Haggai said that God will shake all nations and the desire of all nations shall come. There is no better foundation than the Word of God.

Study to shew thyself approved unto God, a workman needeth not to be ashamed, rightly dividing the word of truth. (2 Timothy 2:15)

God allows certain situations to happen, just to give people a reason to seek His face. Sometimes disasters cause people to seek God with all their heart. God does not give us a spirit of fear, but fear can be a good thing. Some are saved because of fear.

And others save with fear, pulling them out of the fire. (Jude verse 23)

There will be an increase in world disasters, there is no doubt about that. This will include horrific events such as wars, tsunamis, volcanoes, and major earthquakes. Riots, civil unrest, and economic disasters will cause men's hearts to fail. The top scientists are studying extreme weather cycles and preparing for catastrophes. Some of these disasters will happen at the same time in various places. In 2006, I received a prophetic vision of several terrorist attacks occurring across the USA. I saw explosions happening one after another. It looked like six to eight blasts from California to the East coast. I also saw looting and turmoil in the streets. We need to be prepared for a shaking that is about to take place. God will protect and provide for His people even in troubled times. There is a financial shift in progress. The world will see God's people blessed.

The wealth of the sinner is laid up for the just. (Proverbs 13:22)

Behold, I give unto you power to tread on serpents and scorpions, and over all the power of the enemy: and nothing shall by any means harm you. (Luke10:19)

And I will shake all nations, and the desire of all nations shall come. (Haggai 2:7)

When the Hebrews finally came out of Egypt, (Goshen I) they took the Egyptians' gold, silver and clothing. They left Egypt with perfect health, freedom and great financial blessings. They didn't know what to do with the sudden prosperity, and eventually made a golden calf. We need to help the poor and the homeless, but we need finances to do it. God will make a way for those that are faithful in tithes and offerings. God will finance His end time revival. As God puts finances in your hands, use it to win souls. The Bible tells us that money answers all things, but the love of money starts a downward fall. Those who are faithful in the small things, God will make masters over great things. Even the poor of this world are rich in faith. The Spirit of God is searching to find people that will

16

be faithful in all areas. We are entering into the next great move of God. The Lord will go before us and devour our enemies. We will raise the dead, cast out devils, and heal the sick in His name. All things are possible to them that believe.

Gifts of God

God is pulling the veil back and searching our hearts. God is revealing some things and some may be found ashamed. God does not want His people to be double minded.

Paul said, **"Let us hold fast the profession of our faith without wavering" (Hebrews 10:23a).**

The precious blood of Jesus will cleanse and bring restoration to those who repent. I believe God wants to help people start over and forget the past. The glory of God will come upon anyone who repents. The Holy Spirit will return to the prodigal children who have walked away, but chose to come home. Everyone has fallen short of the glory of God. No one has been perfect. The gifts and callings of God are without repentance. God will not take His gifts back once He gives them to you. A lot of singers and musicians were anointed and gifted while growing up in church. Many people have been gifted to teach and preach, but today, they are singing in the night clubs. Even though these people stopped serving God, those gifts are still with them. We should use our gifts and talents for Jesus, not for the devil. Don't allow your gifts to remain dormant either. The Lord wants everyone to use their gifts for Him. God blesses us with abilities and then rewards us for using them. Ask God to increase your gifts.

And behold, I come quickly; and my reward is with me, to give every man according as his work shall be. (Revelation 22:12)

If we don't want to stand before the Lord empty handed one day, then we must start witnessing, preaching, and winning lost souls. We will be rewarded for all of our efforts. If we will stay the course, we will see a harvest. Start planting seed into the hearts of your family and friends. Tell everyone you see that Jesus is coming back soon.

Enlightened by the Spirit

When the Spirit of God begins to enlighten you on upcoming events, relax and soak it all up. Wait on the Lord to give you scripture to backup what you hear. The Lord is looking for people that will draw close to Him and do His will. Those that have a relationship with Jesus, usually have an idea of His plans to direct their paths. Everyone needs clear direction and He will lead us into all truth.

Howbeit when he, the Spirit of truth, is come, he will guide you into all truth: for he shall not speak of himself; but whatsoever he shall hear, that shall he speak: and he will shew you things to come. (John 16:13)

Jesus mentioned events that will happen in the future to give us confidence He is the Messiah. He prophesied events in advance, so that when they came to pass, we would believe.

And now I have told you before it come to pass, that, when it is come to pass, ye might believe. (John14:29)

God Warns His People First

We have verified that the Holy Spirit is still here and working in the body of Christ. The Holy Spirit will teach, reveal, and guide you into all truth. This applies to end time prophecy as much as anything else. God is raising up a mighty army to march through the land. God's lambs are sent out with a prophetic voice.

Surely the Lord God will do nothing, but he revealeth his secret unto his servants the prophets. (Amos 3:7)

The Lord desires to share His secrets with His servants the prophets. God does this by His Word,

19

His voice, and His Spirit. God's people are a prophetic voice that warns every generation. God always warns people when He has had enough. He warned the people in Noah's day, and even the animals had enough sense to avoid disaster. God warned the people in Abraham's day, Jacob's day, and Jeremiah's day.

God is warning people now through His servants that His wrath will be poured out one day upon a wicked generation. It is God's will for everyone to receive the promise of salvation. God has not appointed His people to face His wrath. The people were partying while the animals were boarding the Ark for safety. Often people can not see the signs of destruction approaching. No one thinks it will happen to them or even in their lifetime.

Chapter Two

Signs of Jesus' Return

Knowing this first, that there shall come in the last days scoffers, walking after their own lust, and saying, where is the promise of his coming? For since the fathers fell asleep, all things continue as they were from the beginning of the creation. (2 Peter 3: 3, 4)

Many people today laugh and scorn when a Christian mentions the coming of the Lord. The heathen laughed at Noah building an ark, until the rain began to fall. Some people will always wait until it's too late.

For as in the days that were before the flood they were eating and drinking, marrying and giving in marriage until Noah entered in the ark, and knew not until the flood came and took them all away; so shall also the coming of the Son of Man be. (Matthew 24:38, 39)

Many people will be swept away by the floods of adversity in these last days. Don't allow scoffers to stop you from warning this generation to flee God's wrath. Jesus is coming and we are the generation that shall see Him. With the help of satellite television, everyone can easily see these events in various places at the same time. In the year 2000, the United Nations established and developed a new organization called the United Religions Organization. Their purpose is to stop ethnic and religious wars. This organization will establish a one world religious system operated by the False Prophet. The Antichrist (world political leader) will work with the false prophet (world religious leader) in the new world order. This is man trying to establishing his own salvation.

Great Earthquakes

We have all seen an increase in earthquakes, diseases, fires, and floods. One side of the earth seems to be burning up while the other side is under water. AIDS, pneumonia, venereal diseases, swine flu and strains of staff infections are now out of control. Great earthquakes are occurring almost every month. There have been more earthquakes in the past 100 years than in the previous 500 years added together. From January1, 2010 to May 2010, there had already been over 6700 earthquakes with over 225,000 people killed. No place is exempt in these last days. We have watched rescue teams work world wide trying to help those overwhelmed by disasters. We watched reports of a tsunami that killed over 300,000 people in Indonesia. Many people believe California will face a Tsunami or a major earthquake before the end of 2012. The year

2012 could have several disasters because of the alignment of our planets along with the twelve constellations. I will explain more about 2012 in a later chapter. Scripture reveals that there will be several major earthquakes during the tribulation period that will totally change the Earth.

And I beheld when he had opened the sixth seal, and, LO, there was a great earthquake; and the sun became black as sackcloth of hair, and the moon became as blood. (Revelation 6:12)

And the angel took the censer, and filled it with fire of the altar, and cast it into the earth: and there were voices, and thunderings, and lightnings, and an earthquake. (Revelation 8:5)

And the same hour was there a great earthquake, and the tenth part of the city fell and in the earthquake were slain of men seven thousand. (Revelation 11:13)

And the temple of God was opened in heaven, and there was seen in his temple the ark of his testament: and there were lightnings, and voices, and thunderings, and an earthquake, and great hail. (Revelation 11:19)

The final earthquake will occur when Jesus comes back with all His saints and puts His feet on the Mount of Olives at the battle of Armageddon. This happens at the end of the great tribulation period.

There were voices, thunders, and lightnings; and there was a great earthquake, such as was not since men were upon the earth, <u>so mighty an earthquake</u>, and so great. And the city was divided into three parts. (Revelation 16:18,19a)

And his feet shall stand in that day upon the mount of Olives, which is before Jerusalem on the east, <u>and the mount of Olives shall cleave in the midst</u> thereof toward the east and toward the west, and the LORD my God shall come, and all the saints with thee. (Zechariah 14: 4, 5)

The saints will have to be in heaven with Jesus for them to come back to Earth with Him. Some things are just self explanatory. I realize there are some saints already in heaven, but I also plan on being in this army.

Millennial Reign

We will come back to Earth and enter a one thousand year Millennial Reign with Christ Jesus. We will be kings and priest in the Millennial Reign. If we are faithful over small things, He will make us masters over big things. Thank God, Jesus will return and restore all things. This is when the devil is thrown in a pit for 1000 years. The two men used as the antichrist and the false prophet will be thrown in the lake of fire, and never heard of again. The Devil will be released from his prison for a short time at the end of the Millennial Reign. He will make war one last time (Gog II) and then be cast into the lake of fire forever. (Revelation 20: 1-10)

False Prophets

For there shall arise false Christs, and false prophets, and shall shew great signs and wonders; inasmuch that if it were possible, they shall deceive the very elect. (Matthew 24:24)

It is impossible to deceive the very elect. Those who understand the Word of God will not be misled. The New Age ideas of philosophy are sweeping America. Their ideas of worship and using crystals and meditation to become channels to the spirit world are influencing thousands. Terrorist groups are using world governments and religion to promote hatred toward Jews and Christians. Since 9/11, we have been searching for these terrorist groups and destroying them. Many people gather at auditoriums and pay to hear demon possessed people channel and prophesy smooth words to them. Some religions teach that torture and pain are the way to God. They walk on coals of fire, glass, and nails hoping to find favor. Jesus is the only way to God, and He does not torture His people. Jesus is the door and our only access to heaven. Only through faith in Him, are we saved.

Verily, verily, I say unto you, He that entereth not by the door into the sheepfold, but climbeth up some other way, the same is a thief and a robber. I am the door: by me if any man enter in, he shall be saved. (John 10: l, 9)

Witchcraft, satanism, and goddess worship are being promoted today like never before. They have become several billion dollar industries. The public schools and military facilities have now become havens for idolatry. The airwaves and newspapers are full of psychic 900 numbers. Some fortune tellers claim to get their readings from Jesus. If we don't know the Word of God, we will be deceived.

There shall not be found among you anyone that maketh his son or his daughter to pass through the fire, or that useth divination, or an observer of times, or an enchanter, or a witch, or a charmer, or a consulter with familiar spirits, or a wizard, or a necromancer. For all that do these things are an abomination unto the Lord. (Deuteronomy 18: 10-12)

Rebellion is the same sin as witchcraft. Don't participate with those that claim to communicate with the dead. Avoid horoscopes, Ouija boards, and cults. These promote power without Jesus. Jesus said many shall come in His name.

A Note on the False Prophet

Satan will deceive billions of people with the help of the Antichrist and the False Prophet. The False Prophet will be a world religious leader that has the backing of the United Nations. He will cause the entire world to worship the Antichrist. He will promote the idea of interfaithism which proclaims any faith will get you into heaven. Anyone that knows the Word of God will not be deceived. The False Prophet will have power to make a statue move and speak. This will cause millions of people to be misled. Many already believe in statues bleeding and crying. God said we are not to have any statues or images before us.

And he had power to give life unto the image of the beast, that the image of the beast should both speak, and cause that as many as would not worship the image of the beast should be killed. (Revelation 13: 15)

The False Prophet will work miracles and cause life to enter this statue. This image of the beast will eventually stand in the new rebuilt temple that the Jews will build on the temple mount. This will be part of the abomination of desolation that Jesus spoke of in Matthew 24:15. Although the devil can perform miracles, so can Jesus. Miracles do follow believers that give Jesus all the credit. The False Prophet will promote himself and the Antichrist. He is allowed by God to create miracles to deceive the world. He will tell everyone that the antichrist is the savior of the world. They will believe the False Prophet because they don't know the Holy Bible. Anyone who does not conform to the United Nation's demands will be put to death.

Lack of Love for One Another

We should be speaking the Word and using our faith and expecting to see miracles. We should be praying in the Spirit and laying hands on the sick. So many churches don't have the power of God working in them. They operate as social clubs not wanting to upset a tithe member. Smooth sayings are the norm in many pulpits. Thank God for all the anointed churches where souls are born again and the sick are healed. Jesus is still performing miracles today. I have prayed for thirty four people that were in comas and twenty have awakened. Ten were brain dead. The power is in the name of Jesus. Miracles and deliverance are free for the asking. The baptism of the Holy Ghost is still available today. Another sign of Jesus' return is so many families are at odds toward one another. Some do not even speak to each other anymore. All it would take is for someone to simply say, "forgive me." Pride always goes before a fall. Many people today are walking around full of bitterness. Prayers are hindered because people choose not to forgive. Satan causes arguments, lies and divisions in many homes and churches. He is the accuser of the brethren. He puts thoughts in our minds, and then accuses us of being evil for thinking such things. There is a warfare that we battle in our minds, but we must take authority over our minds. We must think on things that are true, pure, and holy.

For the weapons of our warfare are not carnal, but mighty through God, to the pulling down of strongholds. Casting down vain imaginations, and every high thing that exalts itself against the knowledge of God, bringing into captivity every thought to the obedience of Christ. (2 Corinthians 10:4, 5)

He that loveth his brother abideth in the light, and there is none occasion of stumbling in him. But he that hateth his brother is in darkness. (1 John 2:10, 11a)

Our brother, according to the Bible, is our neighbor or friend. People are afraid to help each other in this day and time. We are our brother's keeper. The world will know we serve the real God, because we show love toward each other. Love will never fail. The Bible reveals that the nature of people in the last days will be very bad.

This know also, that in the last days perilous times shall come. For men shall be lovers of their ownselves, covetous, boasters, proud blasphemers, disobedient to their parents, unthankful, unholy, without natural affection, truce breakers, false accusers, fierce, hate what is good, traitors, heady, high-minded, lovers of pleasures more than lovers of God; having a form of godliness but denying the power of God. (2Timothy 3:2-5)

These are perilous times in which we live. A man's hand shake used to represent his word. Talk shows are full of sexual perversion and they love to bash Christians. Many times when the Bible is mentioned, slurs and frowns are made. Everyone wants to be politically correct and not offend anybody. We must speak the truth and not be afraid to hurt someone's feelings. The world is going to hell in a hand basket so to speak. Someone ought to care about their neighbors. Sporting arenas are packed out and God is an afterthought. Many people will lose their voice screaming for their teams, but they won't even raise their hands and say "Amen" in church. Nothing is wrong with sporting events or being with the family at the lake, as long as Jesus is not excluded. Jesus is the only thing that can fill the void in our life. Entertainment will always leave us feeling empty. Jesus should have priority in our life and family.

He that abideth in me, and I in him, the same bringeth forth much fruit. (John 15:5)

Dead Churches

Now the Spirit speaketh expressly, that in the latter times some shall depart from the faith, giving heed to seducing spirits and doctrines of devils. (1Timothy 4:1)

There are thousands of churches that are now spiritually cold and dried up. There is no life in them because the Holy Spirit is not welcome. The Holy Spirit will never force Himself on anyone. He will invite us into His presence and heal us from our infirmities. We are told to turn away from dead services. We can have spiritual services and still be in order. We should have freedom to raise our hands and praise God.

Where the Spirit of the Lord is, there is liberty. (2 Corinthians 3:17 b)

Even in America, many people can't worship

freely in churches, because of the religious leaders. A congregation is only as spiritual as their leaders allow them to be. Sometimes it is the other way around. A leader or pastor gets fired up and the congregation votes them out. Many pastors are afraid of losing their jobs, so they simply pacify the people. God needs His servants to stand up for what is right.

I've had pastors and deacons to say I was too spiritual or fired up for them, well praise God! I have been praying in the altars after preaching and the pastors would leave and go out to eat. Thank God they trust me, but I needed some help. Some churches wouldn't know Jesus even if He were to make an appearance and perform miracles.

Clouds they are without water, carried about of winds; trees whose fruit has withered, without fruit, twice dead, plucked up by the roots. (Jude verse 12b)

Our natural minds cannot understand spiritual things. We must become spiritually minded. God is seeking a people who will worship Him in spirit and in truth, not lip service, but with our hearts. Jesus wants to be lifted up in every service. Even if we're not in a church building, we can still praise God. We are the temple of the Holy Ghost. The Spirit of God is where people are praising Him.

Most people love God and they worship in truth, but they don't know how to worship in spirit. They often mock people that do. We can all be forgiven for anything, except blaspheming the **Holy Ghost**. It's a very dangerous thing to make fun of someone praying in the Spirit and speaking in other tongues.

Wherefore I say unto you, All manner of sin and blasphemy shall be forgiven unto men: but the Blasphemy against the Holy Ghost shall not be forgiven unto men. (Matthew 12:31)

People should never say anything against the Holy Spirit. If anyone speaks against Him, we bring judgment upon ourselves. King David's wife spoke against him as he worshiped God. She thought David was dancing to impress the girls. She was barren and childless from that day (2 Samuel 6:20-23). A critical spirit will cause us to be fruitless. We don't know what is in someone's heart, so we can't judge if someone is in the spirit or not. We should not be watching everyone else.

Jews Flooding Back to Israel

The Lord liveth, that brought up the children of Israel out of the land of the north, and from all the lands wither he had driven them: and I will bring them again into their land that I gave

33

unto their fathers. (Jeremiah l6:l5)

One of the most remarkable signs that Jesus is coming soon is the gathering of Jews back to Israel. Israel became a nation once again in 1948 after a terrible time known as the Holocaust. This was prophesied in Ezekiel 37 as God breathed life back into Israel after a valley of dry bones. When the Berlin Wall fell in 1989, it caused problems even in the Soviet Union. When Russia fell, over 250,000 Soviet Jews went back to Israel. Directly north of Israel is Moscow.

God said he would send fishermen and hunters to search for the children of Israel and bring them back to their home land (Jeremiah 16:16). The USA used C-130 cargo planes to carry Jews from around the world back to Israel. These exoduses (which also included Ethiopian Jews) became known as Operation Moses, Operation Solomon and Operation Sheba. God said He would restore the Hebrew language and bring Ethiopian Jews back to Israel to serve Him.

For then will I turn to the people a pure language that they may all call upon the name of the Lord with one consent. From beyond the rivers of Ethiopia my suppliants, even the daughter of my dispersed. (Zephaniah 3:9, 10)

Shall a nation be born at once? For as soon as

Zion travailed, she brought forth her children. (Isaiah 66:8)

Israel the Fig Tree

Jesus spoke about the fig tree shooting forth as a sign to know when the end is near. Most scholars believe Israel is the key to biblical prophecy and I believe this also. We must watch Israel in order to know the signs of the times.

Now learn a parable of the fig tree: When his branch is yet tender, and putteth forth leaves, ye know that summer is nigh: So likewise ye, when ye shall see all these things, know that it is near, even at the doors. Verily I say unto you, this generation shall not pass, till all these things be fulfilled. (Matthew 24:32-34)

God referred to Israel as a fig tree and He said the generation that saw Israel become a nation would see all things fulfilled. Men are referred to as trees in the Bible. Paul said the gentiles were a wild olive tree grafted in.

I found Israel like grapes in the wilderness; I saw your fathers as the first ripe in the fig tree at her first time. (Hosea 9:10)

He hath laid my vine waste, and barked my fig

35

tree. (Joel 1:7)

Israel recaptured Jerusalem in 1967 and made it the capital again for the first time in over 2500 years. The Six Day War was unique in so many ways. Israel had conquered the same territory that Joshua had acquired in his day. Joshua also saw victory on the seventh day. We are the final generation of this dispensation of grace. Jewish people are returning to Israel. When Israel builds their third temple, the left behind saints will witness the greatest revival in the history of the world.

When the Lord shall build up Zion, he shall appear in his glory. (Psalms 102:16)

God began restoring Zion (Israel) in 1917 when England came and liberated them from the Turkish government.

Items Needed to Rebuild the Temple

When Israel rebuilds the third temple, just north of the Dome of the Rock, Jews from around the world will go back to Israel. Groups such as The Temple Mount Faithful and the Temple Institute have recreated the articles needed for temple worship. One group is working to build the temple off site. They hope to move the temple in sections when the time is right. An Orthodox Jewish group found two huge cornerstones from the original rock quarry that Solomon used to build the first temple. They have also recreated the priestly robes, and a seven foot golden menorah. It has been reported that all the vessels needed for sacrificing animals have been re-created and completed. Most of the temple furniture has been completed, including the table of shewbread. Two hundred young Levi priests are now registered through computers by DNA. These young men are being trained to perform animal sacrifices.

The Purple Dye

The shellfish that produce the blue dye needed for the high priest's robe and the tallits have begun to wash up on the Red Sea and the Mediterranean shores for the first time in over 2000 years. These shellfish had been considered extinct until just recently when they were discovered once again in abundance. There are some people that have the ability to produce the dye from these shellfish. The New Testament spoke about a woman named Lidia that was a maker of purple. Maybe these particular shellfish is exactly what she used to squeeze the dye in the process.

The Ashes of the Red Heifer

A pure red heifer is also needed for the Jews to start temple worship. Many people around the world have donated red heifers to help Israel start their own herd. Red heifers are now born in Israel. For the red heifer to be sacrificed, it can't have more than two white hairs extending out of any one hair follicle. It is examined with a magnifying glass. The red heifer allows the high priest access to the Holy of Holies on the Day of Atonement (Hebrews 9:12-14). It is believed that the last red heifer was sacrificed just before the birth of Jesus.

There have been nine red heifers sacrificed since Moses was told to do so in Numbers 19:2. The religious Jews were taught that the Messiah would return at the sacrificing of the tenth red heifer. The next red heifer sacrificed will be the tenth. Are you excited? Very soon, we shall see King Jesus! The head rabbi publicly stated on video that they have the Ark of the Covenant. It was found underneath the temple mount, but they won't reveal it until they have the ashes of a red heifer. The ashes were kept in a copper container wrapped in oil rags. Each vessel of the ashes could last 3 to 4 hundred years. Many top archaeologists are now looking for the last copper container called the K'lal which stored the ashes of the red heifer. The K'lal was last hid around 70 AD. Some rabbis believe that the ashes of the last red heifer should be mixed with new ashes to begin temple worship. The Rabbis hope to have a red heifer that is kosher very soon. The red heifer will be guarded at all times. In

1996, a red cow (named Melody) was born in Israel. Every major news network carried the story. Melody was hid and protected in northern Israel. This cow was later declared ineligible. A new red heifer will soon be available.

Israel Will Sacrifice Animals

The Hebrews performed animal sacrifices on the temple mount before the second temple was built.

From the first day of the seventh month began they to offer burnt offerings unto the Lord. But the foundation of the temple of the Lord was not yet laid. (Ezra 3:6)

The first day of the seventh month is when God told the Hebrews to celebrate the feast of trumpets. Several Messianic Jews (Christian Jews) believe Jesus will return around the feast of trumpets. I will discuss more about this feast in chapter seven.

In the seventh month, in the first day of the month, shall ye have a Sabbath, a memorial of blowing of trumpets. (Leviticus 23:24)

The Orthodox Jews may perform some type of sacrifice very soon. Several different groups have tried before, but their efforts failed. The first sacrifice in the new temple may occur on a future feast day. The Sanhedrin has been re-established for the first time since 70 AD. Several petitions to the High Court of Justice asking for permission to sacrifice an animal near the temple area have been denied. The Sanhedrin had to be re-established before the third temple could be rebuilt. They are the ones who will give the order to rebuild the temple. They also make sure all the biblical ordinances are fulfilled according to the Law. The Israeli government knows that any attempt to sacrifice on the temple mount would cause several security problems or even a war. I recently found out that even the Muslims believe a future war will occur called the battle of Gog.

The Peace Treaty of 1993

The United States passed a law in September of 1993 that animals could be sacrificed in a religious ceremony. It appears the Clinton administration lobbied for this bill, and in return Israel would sign a seven year peace treaty with the Arabs. This is exactly what happened. America promised not to put pressure on Israel when they begin animal sacrifices in the future. We watched the world news as Israel's Prime Minister Yitzhak Rabin and Shimon Peres signed a seven year treaty with Yasser Arafat in September of 1993. I will share more information on Peres later. The Road Map to Peace may be the next seven year treaty signed.

Every time the United States puts pressure on Israel to give up land and property, it cost us tremendously as hurricanes, droughts, floods and fires ravish our country. Hopefully, the USA will stop forcing Israel to trade land for peace.

USA Protects Israel in Tribulation Period

I do believe the United States will help Israel during the tribulation period. Perhaps our fifth or seventh naval fleets are the ships of Chittim cruising in the Mediterranean and The Persian Gulf (Daniel 11:30). The United States of America could be the force that grieves the antichrist. Israel is helped by an Eagle in the tribulation period. The USA is represented by an Eagle in prophecy.

And to the woman were given two wings of a great eagle, that she might fly into the wilderness, into a place, where she is nourished for a time, and times, and half a time, from the face of the serpent. (Revelation 12:14)

The woman is Israel spoken about in this scripture. Israel will be protected for three and one half years. A **time** is one year, **times** equal two years and a **half a time** is one half year. The United States is represented by an eagle, just like Russia is represented by a bear, and Israel by a fig tree. The United States protected Israel in the

41

Persian Gulf War. God's hand is on America because we produce eighty percent of world evangelism and we support the nation of Israel. The letters **USA** are in the middle of the name of Jerusalem. God blesses those who bless Israel.

Israel Will Destroy Damascus

Russia has an agreement with Iran to defend her if she is attacked. Again, I believe Israel will be the one to destroy Iran's three nuclear sites. I believe Ezekiel 38 is about to be fulfilled. Since Iran plans to open the nuclear facilities in 2010, Israel will probably be forced to destroy those facilities in 2010. Israel will then be attacked by the Hezbollah in Lebanon and the Hamas in Syria. Israel will strike back and fire rockets into Lebanon and Damascus, Syria. Israel will hit a warehouse in Damascus that has weapons of mass destruction (WMD) that came from Iraq (Isaiah17:1,3). This facility may be hit by accident, but the Muslims will say that Israel has hit Syria with WMD. Israel destroyed Syria's secret nuclear facility back in September of 2007. Israel will win this war and the world will be amazed.

Behold, Damascus is taken away from being a city, and it shall be a ruinous heap. And the kingdom from Damascus and the remnant of Syria: and they shall be as the glory of the

**children of Israel, saith the Lord of host.
(Isaiah 17:1, 3)**

In 2006, the Palestinians elected the Hamas to rule in Gaza and the West Bank. Israel has to contend with a Shiite group called Hezbollah in Lebanon. The Hezbollah and Hamas are Shiite Muslim terrorists. Israel is surrounded on three sides by religious enemies. Ezekiel 38 says Iran, Libya, Syria, Turkey, Lebanon, and Russia will attempt to destroy Israel. However, five sixths of these armies will be destroyed by God and Israel.

Muslims and Jews also Accept the Antichrist

The Iranian Shiites would love to see Israel annihilated. Iran's president (Ahmadinejad) has publicly stated that he wants to destroy Israel and wipe them off the map. He thinks the Muslim world would accept him as their next prophet called the Mahdi. The Jews and the Muslims are both looking for a world leader and they end up accepting the same person. The Bible calls him the antichrist. Muslims believe that Jesus was a real prophet and that He will return one day. Since the Muslims accept Jesus as a prophet, and He was Jewish, they will accept the antichrist who also will be Jewish. He could be part Jew and part Arab. He may be selected as the Secretary General of the UN and come from Syria. The antichrist

43

must be Jewish for the Jews to accept him. He may be traced back to the tribe of Dan. Jacob called Dan a serpent in Genesis 49:17. Revelation 20:2 says the devil is the serpent.

The Muslims believe the Mahdi and Jesus will work together and convert the world to Islam. They could not be more wrong. Jesus will never promote another religion. Jesus is more than a prophet, He is the Savior of the world. I now understand why all the Muslims will accept the Antichrist. The Antichrist will deceive the Muslims and make them think he is the Mahdi. He makes the Jews think he is the Messiah. God puts people in position to fulfill His Word. The Word declares that God will allow both parties to be deceived, because they don't love the truth. God will harden the hearts of all nations just like He did with pharaoh. The Egyptians saw God's mighty power.

And the Lord said unto Moses, Go in unto Pharaoh: for I have hardened his heart and the heart of his servants, that I might show these my signs before him. (Exodus 10:1)

Barack Obama became the 44th president. I told everyone that he would win, because he is related to the other presidents. God put Obama in office to fulfill certain prophecies. I said earlier that a future Secretary General of the UN could be the man that confirms the final seven year covenant. The next Secretary General will be elected in 2012.

Presidents Related

I have found out that all of our presidents are related to each other. President Obama is a tenth cousin to George W. Bush on Obama's mother's side. During any presidential election, just find out which candidate is related to the other presidents, and it appears that is who will win the election. There is a higher power that is in control. God showed me some prophecies that the last five presidents fulfilled while in office. I will include some things about President Obama as well. The Holy Spirit began with President Carter.

Jimmy Carter was elected the 39th president. Iran invaded the United States Embassy in Tehran and held Americans hostage for 444 days. President Carter sent a secret delta force to Iran to rescue all the Americans. Our helicopters crashed due to sand in the bearings and hydraulic failures. We had to re-engineer our military equipment to work in the deserts. This decision would save thousands of lives in a future war (Operation Desert Storm). This administration helped promote and set the stage for Saddam Hussein to become the leader in Iraq. Saddam soon spent a billion dollars restoring Babylon. The Antichrist may be a future Secretary

General of the United Nations. He may move his headquarters from New York City (Headquarters of the United Nations) to Jerusalem. In Jerusalem, he will sit in the re-built temple and proclaim himself God. He may then move his headquarters from Jerusalem to Babylon. Iraq happens to be the second most mentioned country in the Bible. The move to Babylon is just a possible scenario.

Ronald Reagan was being sworn in as president, when the news came that the Americans were released in Iran. President Reagan was used by God to work with Gorbachev (Soviet leader) to help bring East and West Germany back together. The **wall** came down in 1989. This began the march for European Countries (EU) to come under one umbrella. The EU would become the first of ten divisions that will work with the Antichrist. Mikhail Gorbachev, at a young age, was told he would bring religious freedom to Russia. Reagan and Gorbachev ended another 70 year captivity for Jewish people. From 1919 to 1989, Jews were held captive in what was called the Soviet Union. Jeremiah 29:14 was coming to pass when God delivered Israel and brought her out of captivity.

George H.W. Bush became the 41st president and suddenly, Saddam Hussein over took Kuwait. Bush later took the role of telling the world that Saddam was not fighting against the United States of

America, but against the New World Order. He was declaring the New World Order will soon rule.

Bill Clinton was elected as the 42nd president in 1992. Less than one year later, he convinced the Jews and Palestinians to agree to a seven year peace treaty. Yitzhak Rabin and Shimon Peres agreed with Yasser Arafat at the White House. This event was very prophetic. God allowed Bill Clinton to be re-elected in 1996 to plant the seed of dividing the Temple Mount in Jerusalem. Clinton suggested putting a wall (either with bricks, or UN peace forces) between the Dome of the Rock and the future Israeli temple to be built. This is exactly what Ezekiel 42:20 said would occur one day. No sitting US President or other world leader had ever suggested this before. Bill Clinton was later impeached and should have never been re-elected, but God wanted him in office to fulfill prophecy.

George W. Bush Jr. became the 43rd president in 2000 after the Supreme Court decided he was the winner. Bush's opponent, Senator Al Gore, selected a Jewish man (Lieberman) to be his running mate. We are for the Jewish people, but God did not want a Jewish Vice President in the White House when 9/11 occurred for several reasons. Muslims around the world would not have helped us, and most Muslims would have said a Jewish conspiracy was using the US government to destroy Islam.

Bush was re-elected and the same thing occurred again. John Kerry wanted everyone to accept him as a Catholic Irishman, but he was as much Jewish as he was Irish. His grandfather Fritz Kohn had changed their name from Kohn to Kerry in 1902. Can you imagine the Muslim outcry if we had a Jewish president chasing down Islamic terrorist? God once again protected the Jewish people and allowed the U.S to hunt down the Shiite Muslim terrorists. The Shiites are reaping what they have sowed. They have pursued the people of Israel for years and now they are being pursued. We must all reap what we sow, this is a law of God that will always be in force.

Presidential Curse

The zero curse was scheduled for the winner of the 2000 election. Every twenty years since 1840, every president who was elected or went in office in a zero year, died in office, was assassinated, or had an assassination attempt. People prayed for this curse to be broken, and amazingly, it skipped Bush. Here is the list of presidents that fell under the zero curse every 20 consecutive years. These are the dates they were elected or took office, not the dates they died. 8 presidents are in this criteria.

1840 Harrison....Died of natural causes in office
1860 Lincoln......Shot and killed while in office

1880 Garfield.....Shot and killed while in office
1900 McKinley..Shot and killed while in office
1920 Harding.....Died of natural causes in office
1940 FDR..........Died of natural causes in office
1960 Kennedy....Shot and killed while in office
1980 Reagan......Shot and wounded while in office
2000 Bush Jr......**Skipped**

Barack Obama was elected the 44th president on the bases of change, but with little experience. I still believe God put Obama in office just as he has every president. God is in control of every nation. Americans have become very complacent and idol worshipers. Everything is more important than God. One way God will get many American's attention will be to disrupt their money, resources, sports, partying and pleasures. If people gain the whole world and lose their soul, they have lost everything. True believers are on God's economy. Jesus owns the gold, silver and the cattle on a thousand hills. The wealth of the wicked will be given to the just. The just will use their resources to preach the gospel. It is possible for the zero curse to fall on Barack Obama since it skipped the last president. The curse may be over or it could occur again in 2020. I don't expect to see the year 2020 anyway. I do not feel Barack Obama will stay in office for several reasons. One, he has spent millions of dollars to prevent his birth certificate, school records, and every other record of his life from becoming public record. Several law suits have been filed by various groups, so his records will eventually be revealed. His grandmother in Kenya said he was born in Kenya. A few weeks later she died. His public ratings have fallen sharply, as he transforms America to a socialist health care system.

Obama's Purpose as President

The health care system is about getting people numbered. Almost every person will eventually be numbered by the federal government. The Obama health care includes funding for (Medicaid and Chip - page 2124 & 2151 in the plan.). Maybe the Chip program is just for children and low income families. I think we must look past all the smoke and mirrors. Many states are fighting the health care bill, and they may overturn it. You can Google the phrase "medical implants" and get all the references you want for the radio frequency identification devises (RFID). I can also see that God has used Obama to convince the Islamic world that America does not hate Muslims. Christians love everyone, we even pray for those that spitefully use us. The majority of Arabs are Muslim, and since President Obama appears to be Muslim, this has to help our soldiers in Muslim countries. Our prayers have been protecting the American soldiers in a hostile environment. Our soldiers minister about Jesus around the world. The Sunni Muslims are grateful to our soldiers for bringing down the harsh rule of the Shiite Muslims. Maybe God is using reverse psychology on the Muslims by allowing us to have a president that either is or appears to be Muslim.

A news reporter asked a group of young boys in Iraq what they thought of the U.S. Soldiers in their country. One boy said now that the Americans are in Iraq, the people can be Christian. The news man asked what was the difference between being a Muslim and a Christian. The boy said, "Now that I'm a Christian, I can feel God." The news man was totally shocked. I thought about how God said He would speak out of the mouth of babes.

Obama will do several strange things while he is in office. He will weaken the sovereignty of the United States in the eyes of other countries. He may cause the union of the United States, Mexico, and Canada to become one entity with one currency. We are fast headed toward becoming the next European Union. Our new currency may be called the Amero Dollar. America is headed for an economic collapse and more terrorist attacks. If something happens to Obama, another civil war could occur. Our freedom is at stake if we don't rise up and take dominion over wickedness. Sin is running rampant and Christians have been afraid to speak out. People now appear ready to fight for freedom and less government. Obama's health care plan will cause our country to stay in debt. New Senators and Congressmen will soon be elected. Government officials should have the same health system as everyone else and then we would see great coverage.

God is still in control and He did not allow Sodom to be destroyed until the righteous were taken out. The main prophetic reason Obama is in office could be to allow Israel to fight the first battle of Gog by themselves. Bush protected Israel with the Patriot Missile, but this time Israel will protect themselves with their own new missile called the ARROW.

Obama seems to cater to the Muslim world, but Israel and God will be glorified in this next war (Ezekiel 39:21). God will magnify Himself among the heathen, just because He can. The Palestinians want Jerusalem, but they don't want the Jews near the Temple Mount. If Obama turns against Israel and forces them to divide Jerusalem, then America may be divided, either by a terrible earthquake, civil war, or some other disaster.

The Temple Mount

Some believe that the Dome of the Rock must be

destroyed before the third temple is built, but this is not true. No scripture in the Word of God says anything about destroying the Dome of the Rock, but it could happen. Professor Kaufman at Hebrew University discovered that the Dome of the Rock is not the exact site where Solomon's temple was. I believe the Holy Spirit revealed to me that the distance where Abraham offered Isaac and where the ram was caught in the thicket (Genesis 22), is the same area between the Dome of the Rock and the Holy of Holies in Solomon's temple. There are prophecies that state the temple area will be divided. It will happen, but woe unto him that causes it to happen. Hopefully, our government does not force this event to happen. A wall will be placed between both temples to try and please the Jews and Muslims.

But the court which is without the temple leave out, and measure it not; for it is given unto the Gentiles. (Revelation 11:2)

God said a wall shall be placed between the Jewish temple and the profane place (Dome of the Rock). So in retrospect, the Arab mosque does not have to be removed for Israel to have a temple and perform animal sacrifices.

He measured it by the four sides: it had a wall round about, five hundred reeds long, and five

hundred broad, to make a separation between the sanctuary and the profane place. (Ezekiel 42:20)

It is possible for a group to attack the Dome of the Rock thinking it must be removed. Since we are the temple of the Holy Ghost, we don't need a temple in Israel to worship God. We offer up sacrifices of praise and shouts of joy. Jesus will accept our sacrifice of worship because we are His disciples. He has written His covenant and laws in our hearts and minds.

A Word on the Battle of Gog

And seven months shall the house of Israel be burying of them, that they may cleanse the land. (Ezekiel 39:12)

When the war of Ezekiel 38 (Gog I) is over and the next seven year peace treaty is signed, Israel will have to cleanse the land for seven months. It is possible that some type of radiation could be released. An Iraqi general (General Sada) defected to America and said Iraqi soldiers loaded 55 gallon barrels of poisoned chemicals in two commercial airplanes. Both of these planes were then flown into Damascus, Syria. I have already said how Damascus will be destroyed when Israel fires rockets in response to Syrian attacks. A warehouse will probably be hit that is storing barrels of chemical and biological weapons that came from Iraq. A cloud of smoke from poisoned gas will fill the air in Damascus. Thousands of people could die from these explosions and the world will be very angry with Israel. It will be Syria's fault for storing these weapons in an unsafe area. Ezekiel 39:9 says Israel will destroy captured weapons for seven years. It is interesting that the tribulation period will last for seven years.

The Giant Birds of Gog

Thou shalt fall upon the mountains of Israel, thou, and all thy bands, and the people that is with thee: I will give thee unto the ravenous birds of every sort, and to the beasts of the field to be devoured. (Ezekiel 39:4)

I have seen these giant birds in the valley of Hamongog on video. This is the place where the armies of Gog are destroyed. The Israeli scientists say these giant birds are only in this particular valley. Some people claim that these birds are laying a lot more eggs than normal and are multiplying at an incredible rate.

Several Battles Called Gog

It appears to me that there are three battles in the

Bible referred to as the Battle of Gog. Vultures will devour the flesh after the battles of Gog I and II (Ezekiel 39:4, Ezekiel 39:17-29 and Revelation 19:17-21). There are two battles of Gog mentioned in Ezekiel Chapter 38 and Chapter 39. One battle is before the tribulation period and the other is after the tribulation period. The third battle of Gog is after the Millennial Reign (Revelation 20:8).

Most people have never seen this and are confused about when these wars occur. When Gog I ends, Israel will begin to burn weapons for seven years just as the tribulation period begins (Ezekiel 39:9). Gog II occurs at the end of the tribulation period also known as Armageddon (Revelation 19:17-21). Birds will eat the carcass of solders at Gog I and Gog II (Ezekiel 39:4 and Revelation 19:17-21).The birds will not gather at Gog III (Revelation 20:8) which occurs after the Millennial Reign. It will not take 7 months to cleanse the land at Gog II or Gog III because Jesus will restore all things immediately.

Satan Released from Prison

We will enter New Jerusalem at end of the Millennial Reign. Therefore, most of the scriptures at the battle of Gog I in Ezekiel 38 and 39 must occur before the tribulation period. This gives Israel and the United Nation forces time to clean up and restore order. There are some scriptures in these chapters that are fulfilled at the Battle of Armageddon (Ezekiel 39:4,17-29). **Most people have not noticed that Ezekiel chapters 38 and 39 explain the events of two wars.** The Word tells us that Satan will be released at the end of the Millennial Reign to cause wars again. This is why there is another battle of Gog. Most people do not like the idea of Satan being allowed to run loose again, but God has control of him. This will weed out the rest of the bad seed on earth. Satan has one more chance to deceive the nations. He will tempt those that have never been tempted before. Satan will try to out smart God again, but he will fail.

And when the thousand years are expired, Satan shall be loosed from his prison, And shall go out to deceive the nations, which are in the four quarters of the earth, Gog and Magog, to gather them to battle. (Revelation 20:7-8)

The end of the Millennial Reign will allow New Jerusalem to come down from the third Heaven.

A Word on New Jerusalem

God will be the light source of that city and there will be no more wars or sickness. This city comes down after the White Throne Judgment. It will be fantastic to live in a city made of pure gold.

And I saw a new heaven and earth: for the first heaven and the first earth were passed away; and there was no more sea. And I John saw the holy city, New Jerusalem, coming down from God out of heaven. (Revelation 21:1, 2)

And the building of the wall of it was of Jasper, and the city was pure gold, like unto clear glass. And the street of the city was pure gold, as it were transparent glass. (Revelation 21: 18, 21)

And the city had no need of the sun, neither of the moon, to shine in it: for the glory of God did lighten it, and the Lamb is the light thereof. (Revelation 21:23)

This is a real place that God's people shall dwell in forever and ever. This will be the perfect habitat of all time. I am glad my name is written in the Lamb's Book of Life. There will be no more devils when we enter New Jerusalem. Everyone will live in peace, love and harmony forever.

Water in the Desert

The wilderness and the solitary place shall be glad for them; and the desert shall rejoice, and blossom as a rose. It shall blossom abundantly, and rejoice even with joy and singing: the glory of Lebanon shall be given unto it, the excellency

of Carmel and Sharon, they shall see the glory of the Lord. And the parched ground shall become a pool, and the thirsty land springs of water. (Isaiah 35:1, 2, 7a)

In the northern part of Israel, drilling has been done to find water. An artesian well has sprung forth and the desert is blossoming once again. Israel is irrigating water into the desert, growing fruit, flower gardens, and vegetables. The mention of Lebanon in Verse two represents Cedar trees. Solomon brought Cedars out of Lebanon for the first temple to be built (I Kings 5:5-8). Cedars are growing in Israel in the heat of the desert. Carmel was a city known for her fruit, and Israel has a tremendous fruit crop now. Israel has exported some fruit with Carmel stamped on it. Sharon was a city known for her flowers as it was usually covered in rose gardens. Jesus is called the Rose of Sharon (Song of Solomon 2:1). Israel has beautiful flower gardens blooming all over the country side. These events are happening because of the pool of water that has sprung forth in the desert and God's timing.

The Dead Sea

One day people will live along the coast of the Dead Sea called Engedi. They will catch fish from the Dead Sea (Ezekiel 47: 8-11). The Dead Sea is

33 percent salt and minerals. There are currently no fish in the Dead Sea, but one day there will be.

During the Millennial Reign, half of the Dead Sea will be healed and the other half will remain full of salt. Fishermen will catch an abundance of fish in half of the Dead Sea. The Dead Sea is shrinking and already becoming two seas. A vehicle can now drive across the Dead Sea from Israel to Jordan. I have seen it with my own eyes from the top of Masada. Ezekiel 47 speaks of the Dead Sea partially drying up and one half being healed. This event is not supposed to even happen until the Millennial Reign begins, but it has already started. John said he saw a pure river flowing out from the throne like Ezekiel did. John saw the tree of life on both sides of the street, the 12 types of fruits, and the leaves for the healing of the nations. The Bible says in Revelation 22:1-4 and Isaiah 35:3-10 that God will come and save his people. Then the blind will see, the lame will walk, and the tongue of the dumb will be loosed, causing all to be healed at once. There will be no sick people dying. Living waters will flow one day from the Millennial Temple. People are healed today because Jesus is He is the Living Water.

The Sanhedrin Re-Established

The New Sanhedrin reconvened in 2005 for the

first time since 70 A.D. They meet once a month to discuss the rebuilding of the temple and animal sacrifices. Their purpose is to verify the priesthood of the Levites and perfect the art of animal sacrifice. They also insist that the temple must be built exactly the way God said to build it. The temple cannot be rebuilt without the Sanhedrin. The main Orthodox priest appointed seventy one leading rabbis to establish the Sanhedrin. They are the highest rule concerning the laws of the Old Testament. It's their belief that the temple must be built quickly to prevent a major Catastrophe in the Middle East. They have agreed on the location which is about seventy five yards north of the Dome of the Rock. It is amazing how close we are to the beginning of the tribulation period. Israel knows that God is on their side and they will win any battle they face. They know their next battle will be against the Iranians, Syrians, Lebanese, and Russians. However, they also know they will win.

The Euphrates River Dries Up

At the end of the tribulation period, when the battle of Armageddon takes place, the Bible says the Euphrates River will dry up to allow the kings of the east to invade Israel. This 2400 year old prophecy became real due to Turkey's ability to push a button and stop this river from flowing. On July 13, 1990 the Indianapolis Star ran an article stating that Turkey will stop the flow of the Euphrates River for one month to allow a diversion plug to be installed in a reservoir. This would also help fill it up. Man can stop the flow of the Euphrates River now with the push of a button. God is giving us clues and signs to encourage us to stay ready. People need to wake up and get ready to meet King Jesus.

And the sixth angel poured out his vial upon the great river Euphrates; and the water thereof was dried up, and the way of the kings of the east might be prepared. (Revelation 16:12)

Many theologians say the kings of the east may come from China to fight against the Antichrist. Whoever it is, an army will cross the Euphrates.

Hubble Telescope

The Hubble telescope was placed in outer space to send back pictures of deep space. It was repaired in December of 1993 as men worked outside the shuttle for hours. It has now sent pictures back from ten to twenty billion light years away. A huge celestial amount of light has been discovered in the northern part of our galaxy. It seems to be moving our way and devouring the darkness of space in the process. Could this be the third heaven with Christ approaching to get his people? John said the light that dwells in Christ will remove darkness. God is light and we are children of the day, not children of the night. God's love in you will make you glow. The Word of God is a lamp that lights up our path. God came from Teman (Habakkuk 3:3)which means the North. Satan said he would ascend into heaven and sit in the sides of the North (Isaiah 14:13). Hubble has taken pictures that give us an idea just how big God is.

Prophetic Cycles in 2012

Some scientists are now saying that the planets and constellations will form a plus sign (cross) in space in 2012 with earth in the middle. Scientists are saying that three unique cycles will occur in the year 2012. One is the twelve constellations lining up in a straight line. This cycle only happens every 13,000 years. Some planets will also aline themselves in a pattern. The second cycle that occurs in the year 2012 involves the Earth circling our Milky Way Galaxy. This cycle only occurs every 25,000 years. The third cycle is the eleven year cycle that involves the sun having polar shifts and extreme solar blasts. These cycles occur in 2012. Some scientists believe these cycles may cause several disasters on Earth, because of the gravitational pull and solar flares. One Scientist said with these cycles coming together, disasters may occur on a biblical proportion. Believers that are looking for Jesus' return, may leave before 2012 even gets here. September 2011 equals nine eleven because September is the ninth month. Israel now celebrates their New Year at the Feast of Trumpets which is the ninth month. September 2010 also equals a 9/11 as Israel will begin to celebrate the year 2011. There may not be any disasters, but if the Shite Muslims have any say so, danger may occur. Perilous times are approaching and times will just get worse as the Apostle Paul said in II Timothy 3:1-9. God warned His people to watch for His first appearance in Daniel 9. The New Testament warns us to watch for His second appearance. Let's look at some other cycles that reveal the time we live in.

The Birth of Jesus

The year 1996/1997 appears to be the 2000th year from the birth of Jesus. The year 1996 was the 3000th birthday of Israel. Jesus was born between three and four B.C. Herod died in 2 B.C. He had all the children killed two years old and under. This puts the birth of Jesus between three and four B.C. We must study to understand cycles of time that reveal prophetic pictures and events. The Pharisees knew Daniel's seventy weeks revealed when the messiah would appear. They did not know the day, but they knew a year. Daniel said the Messiah would be killed after 69 weeks (483 years) after they left Iraq. The Bible says the Messiah's appearance and death would be before the destruction of the first temple. The seventy week prophecy was divided into 3 time periods. It was 7 weeks plus 62 weeks and then finally 1 week. Each week was seven years each. The last week starts when Israel signs a seven year treaty.

Building the Next Temple

Here are two perspectives on the temple being rebuilt. Nimar Darwish, founder of the Islamic Movement in Israel said, "The Mahdi will decide whether or not to rebuild the Temple. If he decides that it should be rebuilt, I will go out to the Temple Mount and help carry the rocks.... As long as there is a Muslim alive, no Jewish Temple will be built on the Temple Mount." In contrast, Baruch Ben-Yosef, chairman of the Movement to Restore the Temple, said in order to rebuild the Temple, "All you need is a Sanhedrin." It is very interesting that the Islamic leader said if their future leader said to rebuild the Jewish temple, he would help. The Jewish leader knows that the temple is about to be rebuilt because the Sanhedrin is re-established.

Remember that Professor Kaufman at Hebrew University discovered that the Dome of the Rock is not the location of the previous Jewish temples. The Jewish temple was directly behind the Eastern

Gate. There's a Gazebo that stands to the north of the Dome of the Rock. It is called the place of the Spirits. Many believe this is the general area where the new Temple will be built. I have stood right there on that site while on tour in 1998 and 2000 and pictured the Messiah being worshiped.

Chapter Three

Rapture or Tribulation Saints

The year 2000 also known as (Y2K) passed without any major computer problems. Jesus said in Luke chapter 21 that one day men's hearts will fail them for fear of things coming on the Earth. Many Christians have departed from the faith and are not prepared for the return of Jesus. A lot of people are at ease and have drawn back from worshiping God in this Laodicean Age. Angels proclaimed that Jesus shall return one day.

Ye men of Galilee, why stand ye gazing up into heaven? This same Jesus, which is taken up from you into heaven, shall so come in like manner as ye have seen Him go into heaven. (Acts 1:11)

Jesus will return like He left, quickly, and in the air. He will not appear in the streets in America, China, or Israel. When He appears, saints shall be caught up to meet Him in the air. Jesus revealed in the parable of the ten virgins that half of the virgins were not ready to meet Him.

Then shall the kingdom of heaven be likened unto ten virgins, which took their lamps, and went forth to meet the bridegroom. And five of

them were wise and five were foolish. They that were foolish took their lamps, and took no oil with them: But the wise took oil in their vessels with their lamps. (Matthew 25:1-4)

Half of these virgins had allowed the oil to run out. Oil in the Bible can represent the Holy Spirit. We are the vessels and the Holy Spirit is the oil. The Spirit will draw us and convict us of sin, but He will not remain in an unclean temple. If we continue to willfully sin, the Holy Spirit will draw back. If we repent and stop the disobedience, the Holy Spirit will abide or live in us. The virgins represent the church. Fifty percent of the church is not ready for Jesus' return. Even Samson did not know when the Lord had departed from him.

And she said, The Philistines be upon thee, Samson. And he awoke out of his sleep, and said, I will go out as at other times before, and shake myself. And he knew not that the Lord was departed from him. (Judges 16:20)

Samson was sleeping with the devil and playing games with his strength. He eventually lost the anointing and he did not even know it. Many in the church today are enjoying the pleasures of sin and shouting at the same time. Jesus told us to be hot or cold so that He could deal with us. The Holy Spirit will convict us, if we have an ear to hear.

So then because thou art lukewarm, and neither cold nor hot, I will spew thee out of my mouth. (Revelation 3:16)

Anyone lukewarm will not repent because they don't believe they need to. They think they are okay and things will continue as before. Some will wake up one day only to realize they are in trouble just as Samson did. Don't be lukewarm!

Saints in the Tribulation

There are some Christians who desire to go into the tribulation period believing they will do greater exploits. They also believe they will survive the worst time the Earth has ever seen or experienced. The Word reveals that two thirds of the population will die during the tribulation period. The one third that is left will go through the fire.

Two parts therein shall be cutoff and die; but the third shall be left therein. And I will bring the third part through the fire, and will refine them as silver is refined, and will try them as gold is tried. (Zechariah 13:8, 9)

Going through the fire is not a fun process. Fire burns all the impurities out of gold so that all is left is pure gold. Since Jesus said He would spew Christians out of His mouth, we can understand another reason why **saints** are in the tribulation period. Some tribulation saints may be bound by addictions, fear, unforgiveness, and fleshly desires, because they don't have a relationship with Jesus anymore. The tribulation saints will be purged and sanctified through many sufferings, because they will not repent and live holy. Smoking, alcohol and drugs are also unholy desires that will prevent saints from being caught up in the next load. They can still go to heaven by dying in the tribulation period for the name of Jesus. We must walk in peace and holiness to see the Lord. People are destroying their bodies everyday. Since Jesus does not smoke, drink, and curse, neither should we.

Jesus will receive a glorious church one way or another. As we become like Jesus, we become free from the lust of the flesh, lust of the eye, and the pride of life. I have had Church folk blow smoke in my face and curse when I explained this to them. Do you think they are rapture ready? Adam committed sin one time and he was removed from the Garden. Obedience is truly God's top priority.

That he might sanctify and cleanse it with the washing of water by the word. That he might present it to himself a glorious church, not having spot, or wrinkle, or any such thing; but that it should be holy and without blemish. (Ephesians 5: 26, 27)

70

And some of them of understanding shall fall, to try them, and to purge, and to make them white, even to the time of the end. (Daniel 11:35)

I beheld, and the same horn made war with the saints, and prevailed against them. And shall wear out the saints of the most High. (Daniel 7:21, 25)

Daniel saw many saints dying in the tribulation period. However, just because people die in the tribulation, does not mean they are cast into the Lake of Fire. Only after the White Throne Judgment (Revelation 20:14,15) are souls sent to the Lake of Fire. However, fallen angels, the false prophet and the antichrist are cast into the lake of Fire earlier. As long as people are alive, they can repent and go to Heaven. The tribulation saints are:

1. Saints that are lukewarm and have drawn back. (Rev. 3:16 & Hebrews 10:38)

2. Christians that are bound by anger, addictions, lust, and who willfully sin. (Ephesians 5:27)

3. Christians that blaspheme the Holy Spirit by speaking evil of the gifts of the Spirit. These people say healing, miracles, and tongues are of the devil. Some people don't know the difference between the the Holy Spirit and the devil.

4. It is possible for those that do not believe in the pre-tribulation rapture to be left behind, since Jesus is coming after those that are looking for Him (Hebrews 9:28). Some people want to go into the tribulation period, because they expect greater rewards. Saints will warn others and be rewarded, but will also be subjected to pain and sorrow.

5. And finally the last tribulation saints (Jewish people) are those that remain under Judaism. They love God and live Holy, but they have not received *Yeshua* (Jesus) as the Messiah. The Jews that survive in Petra will accept Him at the end of the tribulation period. There will be other religious people that accept Jesus also. The greatest revival is during the tribulation period.

They shall call on my name, and I will hear them. (Zechariah 13: 9)

People all over the world will be affected by the mark, name, and number of the beast. Some people will survive the tribulation period, but the things they endure will be horrendous. Death, famines, torture, and disasters will be worldwide.

And it was given unto him to make war with the saints and to overcome them: and power was given him over all kindreds, and tongues, and nations. (Revelation 13:7)

72

The tribulation period is a time for all the Jews, gentiles, and lukewarm Christians to repent and seek God's face. The Holy Spirit will lift up (be removed) and allow people to be tortured and killed to purge them as gold in the fire. The Spirit of God is here now!

Only he who now letteth will let, until he be taken out of the way. (2 Thessalonians 2:7b)

When He (the Holy Spirit) steps back or lifts up, all lawlessness will break forth. Evil will be rampant and martial law will be enforced. The Holy Spirit is the force really holding the devil back. The fired up saints are a force against darkness, but we are no match against the fallen angels. The Holy Ghost Saints will be leaving Earth when the Spirit lifts up. The dispensation of grace will end and a time of judgment begins. God spared His wrath in Jonah's day, but He will not hold His wrath back forever. God is merciful and His grace is available **today** for everyone.

And they that understand among the people shall instruct many; yet they shall fall by the sword, and by flame, by captivity, and by spoil, many days. (Daniel 11:33)

God has made a way for us to have life after death. God has made a way for His people to make

73

it to heaven either before, during, or after the
tribulation period. You must decide which load you
are going in. The tribulation will be a time of death
and sorrow. Jesus said it will be the worst time on
Earth. The last three and a half years of the
tribulation period is the great tribulation. Are you
rapture ready? Just because some people don't like
the idea of people being caught up before the
tribulation, does not mean it will not happen. Just
because people don't believe in Jesus, does not
mean He don't exist. Don't allow unbelievers to
dictate what you should believe in, trust the Word.

Caught Up or Raptured

**For the Lord Himself shall descend from
heaven with a shout, with the voice of the
archangel, and with the trump of God: and the
dead in Christ shall rise first: Then we which
are alive and remain shall be <u>caught up</u> together
with them in the clouds to meet the Lord in the
air: And so shall we ever be with the Lord.
Wherefore comfort one another with these
words. (1Thessalonians 4: 16-18)**

This event is called the rapture, or the catching
away. The rapture (which is an event, not a
particular time) is viewed by many to either occur
before, during, or after the tribulation period.
These 3 views are referred to as the pre-tribulation

rapture, the mid-tribulation rapture, and the post-tribulation rapture. <u>There are scriptures for all three events.</u> Many think that only one event can occur. Perhaps many scholars have overlooked why scripture speaks of three events. It seems obvious that God will rapture people in all three events, although Jesus will only appear two times. He appears before the tribulation period and then at the end of the tribulation period. This explains a lot of mysteries. I will discuss all three events.

The word **rapture** cannot be found in the Bible, it is derived from the words **caught up** in the above scripture. The Greek word for the words **caught up** is *harpazo*. It means to carry off, to grasp hastily. It also means to snatch up, or to depart. The word rapture has been used to describe this event of transporting the saints to meet the Lord Jesus in the air. The word rapture means a happy event. It will be a happy time when we meet Jesus and our loved ones in the air. Paul also said to comfort one another with these words. It is not comforting to tell people that they must survive a horrendous seven year period, while two thirds of the population dies. Does that sound comforting to you? Some people believe the rapture occurs at the end of the tribulation because Paul said the words **(sound of a trump).** There are seven trumpets in the tribulation period. There are 7 distinct sounds from the Shofar (Jewish trumpet). Trumpets can represent alarm or victory. People use an alarm to wake up. There is definitely going to be a lot of people caught asleep. When we that are awake are caught up, we will get brand new bodies.

Behold, I shew you a mystery; we shall not all sleep, but we shall all be changed, In a moment, in the twinkling of an eye, at the last trump: for the trumpet shall sound, and the dead shall be raised incorruptible, and we shall be changed. (1 Corinthians 15:51-53)

Again Paul mentions a trump, but this time he calls it the last trump. The trumpet will sound as this dispensation of grace ends. There are six dispensations from Adam to the beginning of the tribulation period. The next rapture (5TH rapture from Enoch) will end the dispensation of grace and the tribulation period begins. Millions will soon be caught up or raptured to meet the Lord Jesus in the air. Our bodies will then be changed into glorified bodies. **Everyone that serves God will not die, but everyone will be changed.** Two thirds of the population will die during the tribulation period.

Two parts therein shall be cutoff and die; but the third shall be left therein. (Zechariah 13:8)

I would never suggest for anyone to try and survive the tribulation period. I'm looking forward

76

to inheriting a new body that will never be affected by sickness, pain or sorrow again. When we are raptured, we will not experience any of these symptoms again. Our body changes at the sound of the last trump. It will only take a split second for the children of God to be changed. In the twinkling of an eye, or as quick as blinking one's eye, (which is only one hundredth of a second). We must watch and pray because we do not know when Jesus will return. We must be ready when He appears. We must be free from sin. Satan wants us to be bound by addictions and live in immorality. Jesus warned us to watch and pray. It is up to us to live right and keep God's commandments. The cares of this world will spiritually blind us.

And take heed to yourselves, lest at any time your hearts be overcharged with surfeiting, and drunkenness, and cares for this life, and so that day come upon you unawares. (Luke 21: 34)

Luke told us to watch and pray for the Lord's soon return. He believed Jesus could come back in his day and we should also. Many people are spiritually asleep and are unaware that Christ's return is about to take place. The cares of this life and deceitfulness of riches takes the place of our zeal and desire to serve God.

For yourselves know perfectly that the day of the Lord so cometh as a thief in the night. But ye brethren are not in darkness, that that day

should overtake you as a thief. Therefore let us not sleep as do others; but let us watch and be sober. **(1 Thessalonians 5: 2, 4, 6)**

Although no one knows the day when Jesus returns, Paul said that day should not come as a surprise to those that are rapture ready. This is because God has an army expecting to see Him, while others are waiting to see the Antichrist. Many think they are Christians because they have joined a church, yet they are not born again. Many Christians have backslid or stopped serving God. They are not aware of the time in which we live. We understand that the world will not recognize the coming of Jesus, but the Christians should be awake, sober and prayed up. The catching away will find 50 percent of Christians spiritually asleep.

Jesus said when He returns for His people, the world will be just like it was in Noah's day. Now when we think back to Noah's day, we understand that there was no rain falling, nobody getting slaughtered, and no disasters occurring. If there were disasters happening or water was waist deep, then everyone would have entered the Ark. It will be just like that when Jesus returns, which means the next rapture will occur before the tribulation.

Chapter Four

Can Anyone Escape the Tribulation?

Watch ye therefore, and pray always, that ye may be accounted worthy to escape all these things that shall come to pass, and to stand before the Son of man. (Luke 21:36)

Luke told us to watch and pray that we are worthy to escape the tribulation period. He was describing the tribulation events in chapter 21. Some Christians don't like the word escape. We can't argue with God. It is a fact that some will escape the tribulation period and some will not. When people go missing, the world will be on red alert. The United Nation (UN) will force people to take a mark or chip in their hand or forehead. There is new technology now available that uses radio frequency. It is called a radio frequency identification device (RFID).This technology will be used for identification and banking purposes. This is one of the reasons that all televisions had to be switched from analog to digital. The new technology with micro chips and RFID's interfered with the analog signals. In Revelation 13:16-17 we are told how people receive the mark or name of the beast. Many thousands of people have already received a microchip, but it is not the mark of the beast as of yet. Many animals, electronics, and even some automobiles have all been chipped. It will be very important for the world governments to know why people have totally gone missing from the earth. The governments may declare that aliens or UFO'S have removed people called Christians from Earth. Our UFO will be the Old Ship of Zion, Hallelujah!

Many religious groups will proclaim that God is angry with these so called Christians because they preach that Jesus is the only way to Heaven. The gay crowd will jump up and down for joy. The governments of the world led by the United Nations will force everyone to receive the mark of the beast to eliminate fear. The chip or laser tattoo will work as a transponder to locate people. This mark will be used for electronic transferring of funds. Checks or credit cards will not be needed. Most Christians agree that people will go missing in the last days, they just don't agree on when. I will be leaving on the next load - Praise God! I believe that Israel is about to go to war just before the next catching away occurs. This will fulfill part Ezekiel chapter 38. Israel will then sign a seven year peace treaty. I believe there is enough scripture to prove that a remnant of believers will be caught up just before this treaty is signed. This treaty will begin the tribulation period. The first three and one half years of the tribulation will be peaceful for Israel as Orthodox Jews build the third temple and sacrifice animals. The mark of the beast will be enforced upon the world to buy and sell in the new world banking system. This must occur because of all the debt left behind by those that have been raptured. It will cause an economic meltdown. A terrible time of crime and lawlessness will definitely begin. This first three and one half years (42 months) will represent a time of man's wrath upon man. The last three and one half years (42 months) of the tribulation period will be God's wrath upon man. The last three and one half year period is also called Jacob's trouble.

Alas! For that day is great, so that none is like it: it is even the time of Jacob's trouble; but he shall be saved out of it. (Jeremiah 30: 7)

God will soon pour his wrath out on a wicked world. People that follow Jesus will not experience God's wrath. Anyone who receives the mark, name, or number in their hand or forehead will suffer God's wrath. **Some people escape the tribulation period by being caught up in the air.**

Wars and Plagues

The entire book of Revelation describes several calamities such as deadly earthquakes, fires, and even hailstones that will weigh 100 pounds each. Demons are released to torment men upon the

Earth. Many famines, diseases, plagues, riots and world wars will be widespread. A time of great distress will rule as men try to solve the world's problems. Even the sun will scorch men for five months and yet they still will not repent.

And ye shall hear of wars and rumors of wars; see that ye be not troubled: for all these things must come to pass, but the end is not yet. For nation shall rise against nation, and kingdom against kingdom: and there shall be famines, and pestilences, and earthquakes, in divers places. (Matthew 24: 6, 7)

World War I and World War II were very unforgiving as millions lost their lives. Tsunami warnings are now the norm for coasts around the world. Aids is wiping out entire villages in Africa. We are hearing of these events in various places at the same time.

Because thou hast kept the word of my patience, I also will keep thee from the hour of temptation, which shall come upon the entire world. (Revelation 3:10)

One neat purpose of the Bible is to help people know what to do before, during, and after the tribulation. Jesus said He will keep us from an hour of temptation that will try the entire world.

The rapture is a promise to those that have walked the walk, and talked the talk. This is also an opportunity for God to reward us by taking us up before the world's worst time ever. How does God keep us from this hour of temptation? He will catch us up, just like He caught up Enoch and Elijah.

I will discuss next on why God caught Enoch and Elijah up in the air. These two men are a very powerful prophetic picture of what is to come. God will make an escape for a remnant of believers. If you are left behind, don't take any markings in your hand or forehead. We can feel the presence of God right now, but a day is coming when people will not feel His presence. I enjoy getting in His presence and receiving words of knowledge and wisdom. His presence will take us to another level.

Thank God there will be a day when we will see Him face to face. We are joint heirs with Him. We will be rewarded for believing in His power and majesty. Jesus said all things are possible to them that believe. I believe Jesus meant what He said and He said what He meant. Jesus told us to watch and pray that we may be accounted worthy to escape the tribulation period. If we are not allowed to escape, then God's Word would be in error. A remnant must go missing before the tribulation period starts. God is watching over His Word to bring it to pass. The Word will not fail, and it has no mistakes. Read the above scripture again and study it very carefully. It is very biblical to pray for Jesus to come back and receive you. Even John the Revelator said, "Come quickly, Lord Jesus."

Watch ye therefore, and pray always, that ye may be accounted worthy to escape all these things that shall come to pass, and to stand before the Son of man. (Luke 21:36)

A Very Unique Prophetic Sign

This world has gone crazy with men wanting to be women and visa versa. There are gay churches everywhere with gay clergy appointed with ease. A news report in 2009 said that a man was having a baby. He used to be a woman, but he had a sex change. He/she still had her female organs and accidentally became pregnant. What makes this unique is that God ask if a man could travail with child just before he spoke of Jacob's trouble.

Ask ye now, and see whether a man doth travail with child? (Jeremiah 30:6)

We know a man cannot have a child, but God was giving us a sign to watch for just before the tribulation period starts. HIS RETURN MUST BE VERY SOON.

Chapter Five

8 Raptures Beginning With Enoch

The Bible is full of God delivering people from destruction. We can read how God delivered Noah from the flood, Lot from Sodom, and the Hebrews from Egypt. There are many more people who escaped great destruction such as Daniel in the lion's den, the three Hebrew boys from the fiery furnace, and the Jews from Haman. There have been others who were actually caught up and left earth. There will be more people leaving Earth.

Enoch and Elijah

Enoch and Elijah were raptured or caught up to Heaven in the old testament. There are several passages that prove God saves his people from suffering with the ungodly. Enoch walked with God for 300 years after his son Methuselah was born. God eventually caught Enoch up into heaven and he was never found again. Enoch did not know the day he would be caught up, but Elijah did. This is very important in knowing why Enoch and Elijah were caught up to heaven. It is much deeper than them just being considered as the two witnesses. I will now reveal the purposes these two prophets were caught up to heaven. I was amazed by this information, you may be also.

And Enoch walked with God: and he was not: for God took him. (Genesis 5:24)

Enoch walked with God very closely. Some Bible teachers believe that God revealed the flood to Enoch before it happened. Enoch named his son Methuselah, which means - When he dies then shall it come. Methuselah died the very year the flood came. There will be an Enoch group that will leave this earth before destruction comes.

Behold, there appeared a chariot of fire, and horses of fire, and parted them both assunder; and Elijah went up by a whirlwind into heaven. (2 Kings 2:11)

I believe God told Elijah when He would catch him up in 1 Kings 19:12. Elijah was complaining to God about allowing Jezebel to put a contract out on him. He wanted to go on to heaven and not hang around anymore. God spoke to Elijah in a still small voice and gave him some instructions to fulfill before he could leave Earth. When you read II Kings chapter two, you will see the sons of the prophets taunting Elisha who would take Elijah's place. They were asking Elisha if he understood that Elijah would be raptured that day. Elijah must have told the sons of the prophets about his leaving. The reason Elijah knew he would be caught up is because God told him. This is a symbolic picture of a future event. There will be a remnant of people, (I call them the Elijah group) that will be caught up in the middle of the tribulation. This group will know the very day they will go missing. It will be 1260 days from the time Israel signs the seven year treaty. When the last seven year treaty is signed by Israel, it is only 1260 days to the middle of the treaty. The antichrist will break the treaty in the middle of the tribulation period and then sit in the temple proclaiming himself as God. Remember no one will ever know the day when Jesus will return. If Jesus returned for His people in the middle of the tribulation period, then we would know the very day of His return. Since we can't know the very day of Jesus' return, this rules out the church being caught up in the Middle. Now the Elijah group I mentioned, will be leaving in the middle of the tribulation period. God will raise up and seal 144,000 male virgin Jewish men and catch them up in the middle of the tribulation period.

These are they which were not defiled by women; for they are virgins. These are they which follow the Lamb whither soever he goeth. These were redeemed from among men. (Revelation 14:4)

Notice these were **redeemed**, caught up and removed from among men. It is also possible for martyrs that have been killed for the name of Jesus, to be caught up at the mid point of the tribulation with the 144,000. John said a multitude that could not be numbered will come out of the great tribulation period (Revelation 7:14). I will discuss this group next. We can do great exploits now through the name of Jesus. Don't wait until the tribulation period to get saved or work for God. You might die before the tribulation period starts, where will you be then? If someone dies without Jesus, then the Lake of Fire will be where they spend eternity. The great tribulation will be the most terrible time ever on Earth. As I said earlier, two thirds of the population will die during the seven year tribulation period. It will be almost impossible to live. **Saints that enter the first 3½ years will face the wrath of man.** Remember, God's wrath is the last 3½ years of the tribulation period. We can obtain the promises of God by staying faithful to the calling of God

Be ye also patient; stablish your hearts: for the coming of the Lord draweth nigh. (James 5:8)

Everyone does not get a second chance. There is no purgatory or reincarnation. Few people get a second chance after near death experiences. I was raised up from two comas and I want to serve Jesus every day with all my heart. Jesus will return for those that are looking for Him.

So Christ was once offered to bear the sins of many; and unto them that look for him shall he appear the second time without sin unto salvation. (Hebrews 9:28)

God said His wrath will be poured out one day on a wicked generation. Those that have a real relationship with Jesus will escape God's wrath.

For God hath not appointed us to wrath, but to obtain salvation by our Lord Jesus Christ. (1 Thessalonians 5:9)

Salvation means to be born again and have a relationship with the Living God. It means to be saved, forgiven, and redeemed by a higher power. His name is Jesus and He is the only Savior of the world! I have heard of those who promise their family they will go to church the next week and get saved, but then they die just a few days later. Don't put your salvation off any longer, repent right now. We are not promised tomorrow.

Hatred After the Rapture

Then shall two be in the field; the one shall be taken, and the other left. (Matthew 24:40)

During a normal day at work, someone is going to be caught up. During the seven year tribulation period, anyone professing Jesus as Lord will be placed in one of the many concentration camps and eventually killed. Some people will hide out, but anyone speaking the name of Jesus will be hunted down. Why will one person disappear and another not? It is because some people are rapture ready while others are not. Stay alert, sober, and fired up.

And then shall many be offended, and shall betray one another, and shall hate one another. And because iniquity shall abound, the love of many shall wax cold. (Matthew 24: 10, 12)

A lot of people will be mad once they recognize they have been left behind. The news media will not know what to explain to the public. Jesus said the great tribulation would be the worst ever on Earth. The above scripture reveals the hatred even before the great tribulation period starts. There has never been destruction like the world will see during the great tribulation. Two thirds of the population will die. Some people will die because of man's wrath on the world. Others will die when God's wrath is poured out on a wicked world.

For then shall be great tribulation, such as was not since the beginning of the world to this time, no, nor ever shall be. (Matthew 24:21)

Which load are you going up in? Life is full of choices, and some things are worth believing in.

All things are possible to them that believe. Trust the Word of God and believe what it says.

Jesus Caught Up Twice

Jesus was also caught up into Heaven. He was raptured twice. The first time was right after his resurrection. Mary approached the empty tomb and thought He was a gardener. Jesus would not allow her to touch Him because He was about to ascend to the third Heaven to sprinkle His blood on the Mercy Seat in the third Heaven.

Jesus saith unto her, Touch me not; for I am not yet ascended to my Father; but go unto my brethren and say unto them, I ascend unto my Father, and to your Father and unto my God and unto your God. (John 20:17)

The high priest could not be touched for seven days before he went into the Holy of Holies. Jesus ask Thomas to touch His wounds eight days later.

And after eight days again his disciples were within, and Thomas with them: then came Jesus, the doors being shut, and stood in the midst, and said, Peace be unto you. Then saith he to Thomas, Reach hither thy finger, and behold my hands; and reach hither thy hand, and thrust it into my side. (John 20:27)

91

Ascend means to go up. Jesus went to the third heaven and sprinkled His royal blood on the Mercy Seat for our eternal redemption. The second time Jesus was caught up, was after He preached for forty days.

He was taken up; and a cloud received him out of their sight. (Acts 1:9)

The fifth catching away involves the blood bought, fired up, believers in Jesus. This group has a real relationship with Jesus, and not just lip service. They leave before the tribulation starts.

The sixth rapture includes the 144,000 virgin Jewish men that God has sealed to fulfill His promise to Abraham. They leave in the middle of the tribulation period.

The seventh rapture involves the two witnesses, martyrs, and any saints still hiding out. This group is caught up at the end of the tribulation period just before the battle of Armageddon.

The eighth rapture will take place at the end of the Millennial Reign (Revelation 20:11-15). Death, Hell and the sea will give up the dead. This group is raptured to stand before the Lord. They will be judged according to their works. New Jerusalem will then come down and we will enter utopia. See the pattern here of multiple raptures in the Bible? Here they are again in order:

1. Enoch: Did not know the day he would leave.

2. Elijah: Knew the day he would leave.

3. Jesus: His 1st rapture was after His resurrection and before His 40 days of preaching (John 20:17).

4. Jesus: His 2nd rapture occurred after His 40 days of preaching (Acts 1:3, 9). Jesus was taken up in front of His disciples in clouds of Glory.

5. The Holy Ghost fired up Saints: These are raptured before the 7 year tribulation period starts.

6. The 144,000 virgin Jewish men are caught up in the middle of tribulation period.

7. The Two Witnesses, Martyrs, and Tribulation Saints: at the end of the great tribulation period.

8. The final rapture occurs at the White Throne Judgment or at the end of the Millennial Reign.

We will never have to fight a devil again! Are you excited yet? We have something to look forward to. The world has no hope if they choose not to accept Jesus as their Savior. We must warn them and hopefully someone will listen.

8 Raptures and the Hebrew Alphabet

God gave me an amazing revelation about the **eight raptures** and the **Hebrew alphabet**. When compared to each other, they have the same meaning. Did you know that every letter of the Hebrew alphabet has a meaning and represents a specific number. Most people study the Bible verse by verse and chapter by chapter. Those that know Hebrew can study the Bible letter by letter. Most Bibles have the twenty two letters in Psalms 119 between every eight verses. There are a lot of definitions and meanings to the 22 Hebrew letters. I have a 2 hour teaching on all twenty two letters and their meanings. I have shortened the meanings of the first eight letters for time sake. I have tied the meaning of the eight Hebrew letters to the eight raptures beginning with Enoch.

Aleph (1) equals one and means unity. Enoch was the first person caught up. He and God were walking together in unity. All of a sudden, Enoch went missing and no one could find him. He is a perfect example or type for the next (5TH) rapture. People are about to go missing, and not one of us knows the exact day when this event will occur.

And Enoch walked with God:and he was not; for God took him. (Genesis 5:24)

The next remnant caught up will be walking with Jesus in unity just like Enoch did.

Beth (2) equals two and means witness. Elijah was the second person caught up. He had a witness (Elisha) that watched him ascend up to heaven. The second rapture had a witness – Wow!

And Elijah went by a whirlwind into heaven, and Elisha saw it. (2 Kings 2: 11b,12a)

Gimel (3) equals three and means loving kindness and represents the Godhead. Paul said that in Jesus was the fullness of the Godhead. Jesus was the third individual to be caught up. This occurred after His resurrection. Jesus saith unto her, **"Touch me not; for I am not yet ascended. I ascend unto my father, and your father." (John 20:17)** Jesus then went to the 3rd heaven and sprinkled His blood on the mercy seat for our eternal redemption. He then came back and preached for forty days. Jesus is the third entity of the Godhead (The Word of God) and He is in the third rapture.

Daleth (4) equals four and means praise. It also means an open door. Jesus was caught up again after His forty days of preaching. He is the door for us to praise God in the Spirit. Jesus is our only access to Heaven. Jesus came from the tribe of Judah. Judah was Jacob's fourth son and his name means to praise.

And when he had spoken these things, while they beheld, he was taken up; and a cloud received him out of their sight. (Acts 1:9)

Jesus was in the fourth rapture and then the Holy Spirit came back to live in the believers.

Hay (5) equals five and means resurrection, shout, and grace. A remnant of believers (the Enoch group) will be caught up not knowing the day or hour.

Only he who now letteth will let, until he be taken away. And then shall that wicked be revealed. (2 Thessalonians 2:7b, 8a)

We which are alive and remain shall be caught up together with them in the clouds, to meet the Lord in the air. (1 Thessalonians 4: 17a)

Watch ye therefore, and pray always, that ye may be counted worthy to escape all these things. (Luke 21:36)

And unto them that look for him shall he appear the second time without sin unto salvation. (Hebrews 9:28)

There will only be a remnant of the church

raptured, due to sin, habits, and disobedience. This remnant will be fired up, walking in holiness, and having a full understanding of the grace of God. Anyone who teaches that the entire church will go into captivity, will themselves enter into captivity.

He that leadeth into captivity shall go into captivity. Here is the patience and the faith of the Saints. (Revelation 13:10)

Vav (6) equals six and means the number of man. God made man on the 6th day and then He rested. The number of the beast is a mark, name or number that equals 666. The 6th rapture is a remnant of Jewish virgin men that total 144,000. Twelve thousand men from each of the twelve tribes of Israel. It's amazing that the number six represents the number of man and here is a specific number of men that are redeemed from the Earth.

And no man could learn that song but the 144,000 which were <u>redeemed</u> from the earth. These are they which were not defiled with women; they are virgins. These were <u>redeemed</u> from among men. (Revelation 14:3, 4)

This rapture takes place in the middle of the tribulation period when the Antichrist breaks the seven year treaty. He will stop the Orthodox Jews from performing animal sacrifices in the temple.

These 144,000 men will be caught up exactly 1260 days from the signing of the seven year peace treaty. The treaty on the table as of April 2010 was called "The Road Map to Peace." If this is the final title, then we are very close to seeing Jesus.

Zain (7) equals the number seven. It also means completion and rest. When the two witnesses complete their ministry, they are killed and then they are caught up to heaven. The 7th rapture includes the two witnesses, martyred saints and saints still alive at the end of the great tribulation. These are raptured just before the battle of Armageddon.

And when they shall have finished their testimony, the beast that ascendeth out of the bottomless pit shall make war with them, and kill them. And they heard a great voice from heaven saying unto them, Come up hither. And they ascended up to heaven in a cloud; and their enemies beheld them. (Revelation 11: 7, 12)

Cheth (8) equals number eight and means a new beginning. Noah and his seven family members entered into the Ark. God began a new work with eight people. The eighth rapture from Enoch is the White Throne Judgment. This event occurs at the end of the Millennial Reign. First, Satan is released to make war again (Gog III) and then he is cast into the Lake of Fire and never heard of again.

Death, hell, and the sea will then give up the dead and they are judged for their deeds.

And I saw a great white throne, and him that sat on it, and I saw the dead, small and great, stand before God; and the books were opened, and another book was opened, which is the book of life: and the dead were judged out of those things which was written in the books, according to their works. And the sea gave up the dead which were in it; and death and hell delivered up the dead which were in them;and they were judged every man according to their works. And death and hell were cast into the lake of fire. This is the second death. And whosoever was not found written in the book of life was cast into the lake of fire. (Revelation 20:11-15)

The souls that are raised up from death, hell, and the sea are caught up to stand before God. All the people that died from the beginning to this day, that did not serve God, will be cast into the lake of fire. New Jerusalem comes down from the third heaven and we inherit our new home. When we compare the definitions of the Hebrew letters to the eight raptures from Enoch to the White Throne Judgment, we see a very unique pattern. Most ministers have never seen this revelation between the raptures and the Hebrew letters. This is another unique puzzle that only God could have developed with such a beautiful pattern.

Post Tribulation Catching Away

Let's go back and pick up where we had left off on the post tribulation catching away. Those that believe in the post tribulation rapture believe that the rapture of the church will occur at the end of the seven year treaty. This is called post trib- but pre wrath. This is the great tribulation period when the battle of Armageddon occurs. The tribulation period (also known as Daniel's 70th week) is divided into two periods of three and one half years (1260 days each). If Jesus waits until the middle or end of the tribulation period, we would know the very day of His coming.

Given this unique evidence, most will say that those days shall be shortened, and therefore we don't know when he will return. Days are actually shortened for the pre-trib saints. Scripture also reveals that Jesus will return again at the end of the tribulation to destroy the armies at the battle of Armageddon. He will bring His saints back with Him. We must be with Jesus if we are to come back with Him. I say this because I plan on being in this group that Jesus brings back with Him. We will rule with Jesus for 1000 years. We will have jobs to do on this Earth as we rule with Jesus during the Millennial Reign as kings and priests.

Behold, the Lord cometh with ten thousands of his saints. (Jude V. 14 b)
And the Lord my God shall come, and all the saints with thee. (Zechariah l4:5d)

Blessed and holy is he that hath part in the first resurrection: on such the second death hath no power, but they shall be priests of God and of Christ, and shall reign with Him for a thousand years. (Revelation 20:6)

God said blessed are those that are in the first resurrection, so this proves that there will be more than one resurrection. Everyone in the next rapture (fifth rapture) will rule with Jesus during the Millennial Reign as kings and priest.

The Two Witnesses

The two witnesses will prophecy 1260 days and then they will be killed. After three and one half days, they are resurrected and then caught up to Heaven in the sight of millions of people. Every eye will see these two men caught up because of television and satellite.

And they heard a great voice from heaven saying unto them, Come up hither. And they ascended up to heaven in a cloud; and their enemies beheld them. (Revelation 11:12)

101

I believe these two witnesses are Elijah and Moses. Elijah will cause it not to rain while Moses will turn the waters to blood and smite the Earth with plagues. Elijah and Moses did these things during their days of ministry. Moses brought plagues on Egypt and turned the Nile River to blood. Elijah spoke as God had instructed him and caused the rain to stop for three and one half years. It did not rain again until Elijah said so.

These have power to shut up heaven, that it rain not in the days of their prophecy: and have power over waters to turn them to blood, and to smite the earth with all plagues, as often as they will. (Revelation 11:6)

Jesus was transfigured with two other individuals in plain sight of Peter, James, and John. God once again was revealing who the two witnesses are.

And was transfigured before them: and his face did shine as the sun, and His raiment was white as the light. And, behold, there appeared unto them Moses and Elijah talking with him. (Matthew 17:3)

This is very clear evidence revealing the two witnesses. I was amazed when the Holy Spirit revealed this to me. Remember, Moses was buried by God and his body was never found. Satan argued with God to see the body of Moses, but was

102

rebuked by an angel of God. Moses was never seen again until he appeared with Jesus on the Mount of Transfiguration. Peter was an eyewitness that saw Moses and Elijah. He recognized them although he had never seen them before. We will be known by all the other saints. Although we will receive a new name and new body, we are still recognized by our loved ones. Are you ready for that reunion? I am anxious to see relatives that have gone on ahead and received their robe and crown. One day you will receive a robe and crown also.

Repent or Go Into the Tribulation

The church of Thyatira was told by God that He would send them into the great tribulation if they did not repent.

Behold, I will cast her into a bed, and them that commit adultery with her into great tribulation, except they repent of their deeds. (Revelation 2:18-22)

Idols can be anything that means more or takes more of our time than God. This church group of Thyatire had this problem, although they loved God. How much more does God have to say to convince people to live a repentant life, or face severe consequences. **It's very plain to see that God has promised that a repentant people will**

escape the great tribulation period. God must honor His Word. Jesus spoke against most of the churches in the second and third chapters of the book of Revelation. This proves that we all can do much better. Don't get saved and satisfied, get saved and filled with the Holy Spirit. Jesus was pleased with the Church of Thyatira's works, service and faith, but He still found flaws that needed correction. If we examine ourselves, we can see what we need to do to get closer to Jesus.

We That Are Alive

Most Christians believe that Enoch and Elijah are the two witnesses because they were caught up or raptured and never died. Paul said in Hebrews 9:27 that it has been appointed unto man once to die and then the judgment. Since Enoch and Elijah were raptured, they never died. Some teach that they must come back and die. Although Paul revealed that man will die unless he is raptured, he also taught in First Thessalonians that everyone will not die. The dead shall rise first, then **we that are alive** and remain shall be caught up to meet the Lord in the air (1 Thessalonians 4:17). We that are raptured will not come back to Earth and die, just because we never died, and neither will Enoch. Elijah will come back and die along with Moses during the tribulation period. These are the two witnesses as I said earlier. Moses represents a remnant in the rock waiting to see the Glory of God. Elijah represents the 144,000 Jewish virgin men that are raptured in the middle since Elijah knew the very day he would be raptured. These 144,000 Jewish men are sealed by God. There are over a billion people in false religions that teach we must die and be reincarnated through ten lifetimes to get to heaven. Listen, we only have one time to get this thing right. Depending on which rapture you go in, (before, during, or at end of the tribulation), you will not come back to Earth to die just because you never died. No one will be reincarnated either.

I am excited about receiving a new body. The eight raptures found in the Bible is an amazing study. Some people like to include John because he was told to come up hither. I don't include John in the eight raptures because he was only in the spirit. We can also get in the Spirit and experience things that our mind can not comprehend.

The first voice which I heard was as it were of a trumpet talking with me; which said, Come up hither, and I will shew thee things which must be hereafter. And immediately I was in the spirit. (Revelation 4:1-2,)

Although John was told to come up hither, he was in the spirit. His body was not caught up. The

Apostle Paul was also caught up to the third heaven (II Corinthians 12:3,4) but I don't count it in the eight raptures, because it was just his spirit.

And I knew such a man, how that he was caught up into paradise, and heard unspeakable words, which it is not lawful for a man to utter. (II Corinthians 12; 3a, 4)

Paul's out of body experience gave him great understanding. This powerful encounter allowed Paul to obtain knowledge about suffering and humility. He said he heard unspeakable words that man can not utter. We must be in the spirit to have Godly encounters. Paul may have heard angels talking, singing and worshiping God. Later, an evil spirit was allowed to fight against Paul to keep him humble. We can do all things in Christ Jesus, but anything we accomplish is because of Him. The devil can't do anything right, when he attacks, we just pray that much more.

Chapter Six

The New World Order

The next time Israel is attacked, they will not sit back like they did during the Persian Gulf War of 1991 when Iraq bombed Tel Aviv. Israel will strike back quickly. Israel has obtained over four hundred nuclear warheads mostly from the United States. The Persian Gulf War was prophesied in the Bible. Jeremiah 50:9 spoke of an assembly of nations destroying Iraq with arrows. Israel now has a new missile defense (much like the Patriot Missile) called the "Arrow." God said he would send a destroying wind or fanners to conquer Iraq's brigandine (army tanks).

The United States sent the Apache Helicopter and destroyed over 3,000 of Saddam Hussein's army tanks. The fanners wiped out the brigandine just as Jeremiah had prophesied in chapter 51. Israel now has an advanced Air Force with helicopters (fanners) of their own. During the Persian Gulf War (Operation Desert Storm), the United States Army was placed in Saudi Arabia alongside the Syrian and Turkish army. America flew more soldiers and weapons across the oceans faster than ever before. Ezekiel saw Operation Desert Storm happening 2,600 years ago. These amazing scriptures reveal events in my lifetime.

Thou shalt ascend and come like a <u>STORM</u>, thou shalt be like a cloud to cover the land, thou, and all thy bands, and many people with thee. Sheba, and Dedan. and the merchants of Tarshish, with all the young lions thereof. (Ezekiel 38:9, 13a)

The word "ascend" means to take off quickly. The word "storm" became part of the name of the war. "As a cloud," represents by air. "All thy bands" implies the United Nations. Sheba and Dedan is the same nation today called Saudi Arabia. Today the merchants of Tarshish is the combination of Syria and Turkey. America came out of England. England's symbol is a lion. America, Australia, Canada, Ireland and Denmark are "young lions." That is amazing that 2600 years ago the Prophet Ezekiel said the young lions would fight the Chaldeans with the help of Tarshish.

The Young Lions actually killed over 200,000 Iraqi soldiers along side the Syrian and Turkish Armies. I would say that Ezekiel was very accurate to say the least. Since 2003, the United States has been at war with Iraq. Saddam Hussein was removed and executed. His two tyrant sons were also killed. Saddam also killed thousands of his own people just to prove a point. The world does not need these kind of dictators. Now, Afghanistan is also in the war because of Osama Bin Ladin. We are in a spiritual warfare against terrorism, but with Jesus on our side, we will win.

The Beast in the Sea

And I stood upon the sand of the sea, and saw a beast rise up out of the sea, having seven heads and ten horns. (Revelation 13:1)

John also saw the same beast that Daniel saw (Daniel 7:23-25). The seven heads represent seven empires that want to destroy Israel and rule the world. The sixth empire was the Roman Empire. Rome first began around the year 753 B.C. and in the beginning was ruled by seven kings. The people of Rome then rose up and took back control (exactly what America needs to do). They chose a counsel, senate and emperors to rule them. Rome was finally overrun by Barbarians, Germans, and then Persians. Although Rome basically conquered a lot of territory, they chose not to conquer the Persians in Iran which became a grave decision.

This allowed the religion of Islam to be established in the sixth and seventh centuries. Today, the world is still terrorized by Islamic fanatics called Shiite Muslims. Their goal is to either convert every person to Islam or kill them. One Roman emperor, Diocletian, chose to divide the Roman Empire into two empires: The Eastern and Western Empires. The Western Empire was conquered back in 476 A.D., while the Eastern Empire was conquered by the Turks under their leader Mohammed II in the year 1453 A.D. John the Revelator had a revelation that the Roman Empire would come alive again. This new Roman empire is called the European Union (EU). The EU has gained strength and is a model for the world to follow in it's footsteps. The purpose of the Roman Empire becoming a superpower once again will force the world into ten divisions. The EU does not understand this, but it is prophecy coming to pass before our very eyes.

And I saw one of his heads as it were wounded to death; and his deadly wound was healed: and all of the world wondered after the beast. (Revelation 13:3)

The EU started it's come back in 1957 with the Treaty of Rome. It officially came back alive in 2003. The current twenty seven member nations includes (Austria, Belgium, Bulgaria, Cyprus, Czech Republic, Denmark, Estonia, Finland, France, Germany, Greece, Hungary, Ireland, Italy, Latvia, and Lithuania. Also Luxembourg, Malta, Netherlands, Poland, Portugal, Romania, Slovakia, Slovenia, Spain, Sweden, and also the United Kingdom). Several more countries have applied to be included in the EU. This powerful entity (the

EU) is now the world's largest superpower with it's economic and military power. The prosperity of the EU will force the world to establish nine more divisions. John saw this beast rising up out of the sea (which represents people) having ten horns. The ten horns represent ten divisions coming together. Daniel saw three kings being removed.

And the ten horns out of this kingdom are ten kings that shall arise: and another shall rise after them; and he shall be diverse from the first, and he shall subdue three kings.
(Daniel 7:24)

Which three kings are removed is not revealed as of yet. The world will soon be divided into ten divisions. These ten divisions will each have a king or president over them. They will all give their authority to the Antichrist, which may be a future Secretary General of the United Nations. All of the countries in the EU have given their sovereignty over to the president of the EU. When the Antichrist removes three kings, then these seven divisions will become the eighth beast.

And the beast that was, and is not, even he is the eight, and is of the seven, and goeth into perdition. (Revelation l7:11)

The Holy Roman Empire was born on December 25, 800 A.D., when Pope Leo III placed a crown on the head of a man named Charlemagne, saying, "I hereby crown you emperor of the Holy Roman Empire." The Holy Roman Empire ruled Europe through the next 1000 years with the strongest leader and the Pope from Italy (thus the name Holy Roman Empire). The Old Roman Empire was in authority during the days of Jesus, and when John the Revelator wrote his Epistles. In 1993, the European Community (EC) also known as the EU, declared that all nations who traded with it must have a code mark on their products. This mark was a circle with a dragon in the middle. The EU has removed barriers at the borders of these nations to allow traffic among themselves without a passport. Much like traveling from state to state in the USA. Some of the EU currency has a picture of a woman riding the back of a beast. Even the United Nations building in New York has a woman riding a beast in the lobby.

So he carried me away in the spirit into the wilderness: I saw a woman sit upon a scarlet colored beast, full of names of blasphemy, having seven heads and ten horns.
(Revelation 17: 3)

The world will be forced into a one world banking system and a one world religious system. Pope John Paul II, symbolically blessed Mikhail Gorbachev in Russia, thus winning over many of the Russian people to Catholicism. Pope John II made history in January of 1994 by recognizing Israel as a sovereign nation. The Pope also visited Israel in 2000. This was the first time a Pope had visited Israel since 1964. The antichrist will gain world recognition and power and force everyone to receive a mark in their hand or forehead.

The Microchip

A medical team helped develop the microchip that has already been placed in thousands of people. They were trying to develop a microchip that would help cripple people walk. The chip is now injected with a hypodermic needle. The chip will only work in the hand or forehead because of sweat glands. It is one forth the size of a grain of rice. The chemical surrounding the chip (lithium) can leak out and cause terrible sores.

And the first went, and poured out his vial upon the earth; and there fell a noisome and grievous sore upon the men which had the mark of the beast and upon them which worshiped his image. (Revelation 16:2)

Let's examine the name of the Antichrist. This man could be revealed when the seven year covenant is signed. The world will be watching on every news channel. Names have surfaced over the years and put in numerical sequence. Some names have come out to 666. This is the number of the beast. There are two names mentioned in scripture concerning the Antichrist. One is Hebrew and the other is Greek.

And they had a king over them, which is the angel of the bottomless pit, whose name in the Hebrew tongue is Abaddon, but in the Greek tongue hath his name Apollyon. (Revelation 9:11)

These names mean devil, or destroyer. These names may be translated into a numeral value and placed in a chip or RFID. Never receive a mark in your hand or forehead.

And the third angel followed them, with a loud voice, If any man worship the beast and his image, and receive his mark in his forehead, or in his hand, The same shall drink of the wine of the wrath of God, which is poured out without mixture into the cup of his indignation; and he shall be tormented with fire and brimstone in the presence of the holy angels, and in the presence of the Lamb. (Revelation 14:9,10)

Tell everyone you see that they must not take a mark, name, or number in their hand or forehead during the tribulation period. I do not want to receive any kind of mark or chip in my body. Amazingly, there are already over 30,000 people with a chip in their body. The governments of the world have planned for everyone to receive this type of identification by 2017. One day it will be a reality, but I don't expect to be here. If you are left behind, then resist any markings or microchips.

World Computer System

Microchips are now implanted into animals and automobiles (On Star) even as I write this book. These chips identify ownership. Governments of the world are now researching ways to put a chip, or bar code on individuals for banking purposes. Also, when children are born, if a chip was planted into the forehead or hand, a satellite would be able to locate the child in the event they went missing. The armed forces are exploring this option for enlisted personnel to prevent AWOL (absent with out leave) or MIA (Missing in action). The chip is being placed in the top military brass in the event they are kidnapped, or leave the country.

This seems to be a good idea, but when the antichrist takes control, this will be mandatory. The world is approaching a world banking system by means of a "New World Order." Many officials claim this system will be in operation soon. A huge computer system called the Beast, is in

Brussels, Belgium. It takes up three floors of the administration building. Never before has a group of nations had such advanced technology to control the world of trade and identification. Computers can now label people with marks, names and numbers.

A curious fact about the Internet is that no group masterminded it. In the beginning, it had no planning council or board of directors. It simply grew out of the need for global communication. It was used by academic staffs as an inexpensive way for many universities to communicate. Then the business and banking industry caught on. Soon a **network** developed and everyone wanted to be a part. This term was soon shortened to (**the net**). The rest as they say, is history. Eventually, hackers and other devotees soon gave it another name. The net became known as (**the web**). It later became known as the (**world wide web**). Curiously, world wide web was also shortened to (**www**). When you want to contact someone or a business on the Internet, you type the three letters www, followed by a dot, then the specific designator or name.

For instance, you can contact us on our web site at www.rickmadison.org. It is interesting that the English letter <u>w</u> is equivalent to the Hebrew letter Vav. The Vav is the sixth letter of the Hebrew alphabet. It represents the number six. When we type the three letters - **www** - we are entering the Hebrew equivalent of 666. The antichrist will use a global communications system to identify all humans. This system has his initials on it. Many world governments desire to have all humans marked or chipped by 2017. The Obama health care plan may have Americans marked by 2013.

The Bible Code

The computer is also a great tool for ministry. A man named Eli Rips, who many consider as the greatest mathematician alive, used the computer to discover the Bible Code. Mr. Rips, a professor at Hebrew University, used a process known as Equal Distant Letter sequence (ELS). He removed skip spaces between the words in the Old Testament. He and two other Israeli scientists conducted many test and discovered that there are thousands of codes in the bible. These codes reveal every historic event that has occurred in the world. This has shook up the scientific community and most agreed that a higher life source wrote the Holy Bible. They are finally seeing some light.

Sun, Moon and Stars

In 1948, Israel became a nation. In 1957, the Treaty of Rome was signed by six nations (Belgium, Holland, Luxembourg, West Germany,

France, Netherlands) thus beginning the European Community's march toward world power. In 1967, Jerusalem became the capital of Israel, thus ending some of the Gentile rule. In 1969, the USA was putting the first rocket on the moon. In the 1980's, the Soviet Union launched "MIR", a small space orbiting vessel. The USA invented three space rockets called Discover, Challenger, and Endeavor. These are used like airplanes to gather information about gravity, space, science and medicine. Israel became a nation in 1948, then captured Jerusalem in 1967, and then a man walked on the moon in 1969. This order of sequence confirms scripture.

And Jerusalem shall be trodden down of the Gentiles, until the time of the Gentiles be fulfilled. And there shall be signs in the sun, and in the moon, and in the stars. (Luke 21:24)

The gentiles lost some control over Jerusalem in 1967. Man walked on the moon in 1969, just two years after Israel captured Jerusalem .

Immediately after the tribulation of those days shall the sun be darkened, and the moon shall not give her light. (Matthew 24:29)

According to NASA, the year 2014 has two (blood moons) or total eclipses of the moon. One occurs on April 15, 2014 (the Feast of Passover) and one occurs on October 8, 2014 (The Feast of Tabernacles). These two eclipses are followed by two additional (blood moons) in the year 2015. One occurs on April 4, 2015 (The Feast of Passover) and the other occurs on September 28, 2015 (the Feast of Tabernacles).

According to NASA, four total lunar eclipses in a row is known as a **tetrad**. After four blood moons in 2014 and 2015, there are no more tetrads occurring in this century. There have been seven tetrads since the first century. They have occurred on the Feast of Passover and the Feast of Tabernacles. These began in 162/163 A.D., and occurred thereafter in 795/796 A.D., 842/843 A.D., 860/861 A.D., 1493/1494 A.D., 1949/1950 A.D., 1967/1968 A.D., with the eighth tetrad scheduled to occur in 2014/2015 A.D. This is very amazing that these eclipses occurred on Jewish feast days.

There are two solar eclipses in the year 2015. One solar eclipse will occur on March 20, 2015 which happens to mark the first day of the **sacred calendar** for the Jewish New Year. The other solar eclipse will occur on September 13, 2015 which happens to mark the first day of the **civil calendar.** Both of these SOLAR ECLIPSES occur exactly 14 days before the blood moon lunar eclipses.

The Next Rapture

It appears to me that the next rapture may occur

between 2010 and 2018. These eight years will be unique. September of 2011 equals 9/11, because September is the ninth month. In 1917, Israel was delivered from another 400 years of captivity from the Turkish government. The Balfour Treaty was signed by England to help Israel obtain a home in Palestine. The Balfour Declaration was a letter from British Foreign Secretary, Lord Arthur James Balfour to Lord Rothschild. It was delivered to a Jewish Activist named Chaim Weizmann. In 1918, the Jewish people tasted freedom once again. One hundred years later, the year 2018 appears to be very significant. Remember one hundred years was a generation in Abraham's day (Genesis 15:13-16).

Seventy Year Cycle

The days of our years are threescore and ten. (Psalms 90:10)

A score equals twenty years, thus three score is sixty years and by adding ten years to it, we have seventy years. Israel became a nation in 1948. By adding seventy years for a righteous generation, we arrive at the year 2018. Imagine the celebration when Israel has been a nation seventy years (1948-2018). There is a reason the Psalmist said the days of our life are 70 years. Many people believe we are only promised seventy years, but it can't mean that because there are people that are a 100 years old or older. I believe it is a prophetic statement concerning the nation of Israel.

Mystery of the Hours

There are two kinds of time in the Greek. Remember the New Testament was written in Greek. One source of time is the Karros and the other is the Chronos. The Karros is a season of time such as Solomon explained in Ecclesiastes chapter three. There is a time for peace and a time for war; The Chronos is a specific time to attend something such as work, church, or to fulfill an appointment.

In Matthew 20:1-6, JESUS HIRED LABORS AT SPECIFIC HOURS for certain reasons. The sequence of hours that Jesus hires labors is a prophetic picture of events in our walk with Him and His return. For instance, Jesus hires labors at the **third hour**, the **sixth hour**, the **ninth hour** and the **eleventh hour** (Matthew 20:3-5). There is a revelation of experiences in each of these hours. First we must become labors or disciples in the kingdom of God. Once we are born again, we can expect a huge payday called eternal life. **The third hour** experience is being filled with the Holy Spirit. The 120 people that were filled in the upper room were accused of being drunk. Peter stood up and said they were not drunk, because it was just the **third hour** of the day (Acts 2:15). The third hour visitation is being filled with the Holy Spirit. The next hour of visitation is **the sixth hour**

121

experience. It is found in (John 4: 6 ,21, 22, 23) as Jesus turns a four time divorced woman into a true worshiper. She caused many Samaritans to get saved. God can use anybody regardless of their past. The sixth hour experience is learning to worship God in Spirit and in truth. **The ninth hour** experience in God is walking in the supernatural. Signs and wonders follow them that believe. Peter and John saw a crippled man healed at the ninth hour (Acts 3:1, 7, 8). **The Eleventh hour** is a prophetic sign of God's time clock. The reason God did not hire anyone at the twelfth hour is because there is a rapture at the twelfth hour.

And at midnight there was a cry made, Behold the bridegroom cometh. (Matthew 25:6)

The people shall be troubled at midnight, and pass away:and the mighty shall be taken away without hand. (Job 34:20)

I believe God's clock has 11:59 pm on it, Are you able to hear the midnight call? Jesus said to work while it is day, for night is approaching. Every clock has a twelve on it. One place in the world it is noon and the other part of the world it is midnight. Get ready to hear the midnight call.

Chapter Seven

Seeing in the Spirit

God is raising up an army of believers. They are marching through the land. They will not break rank or be disobedient. If we walk in the spirit, we will live in the spirit. The traditions of men, and a lack of hunger for the deep things of God, keeps many people from seeing, hearing, and moving into the spiritual realm. God wants your eyes and ears to experience the supernatural.

But blessed are your eyes, for they shall see: your ears, for they shall hear. (Matthew 13:16a)

That the God of our Lord Jesus Christ, the Father of glory, may give unto you the spirit of wisdom and revelation in the knowledge of him, That the eyes of your understanding being enlightened; that ye may know what is the hope of his calling. (Ephesians 1:17, 18a)

In II Kings chapter 2, the sons of the prophets were following Elijah and Elisha from city to city. Elisha wanted a double portion of the anointing from Elijah. The sons of the prophets did not want a double portion of the anointing. They actually made fun of Elisha for believing that he could receive more of the anointing. They tried to make him doubt he was going to receive anything. Elisha followed Elijah from Gilgal to Bethel, then to Jericho then to Jordan. Gilgal means to put away the flesh, while Bethel means the house of God. Jericho means victory and shouting, while Jordan means freedom and sanctification. Elijah wanted Elisha to be content at each city. One reason many Christians don't walk in the spirit is because they are satisfied with what little anointing they have already received. Thank God for salvation, it is the most important event in a person's life. However, a Christian should be able to raise their hands and praise the Lord without fear and intimidation.

Many Christians need deliverance from tobacco, alcohol, jealousy, lust and anger just to name a few. God wants to deliver multitudes that are in the valley of decision. Everyone wants something, but what they need is more of God. When Elijah was caught up, Elisha saw in the spirit realm.

And it came to pass, as they still went on, and talked, that, behold, there appeared a chariot of fire, and horses of fire, and parted them both asunder; and Elijah went up by a whirlwind into heaven. (II Kings 2:11)

The sons of the prophets are similar to many Christians of today. They were watching from a distance wondering what would happen. People will always stay in the back and watch. Many criticize and question if what is happening is real.

And when the sons of the prophets which were to view at Jericho saw him, they said, The spirit of Elijah doth rest on Elisha. And they came to meet him, and bowed themselves to the ground before him. (2 kings 2:15)

The sons of the prophets did not see the horses and chariots of fire. True believers will see and hear spiritual things that the majority never experience. They were in such unbelief that they sent a search party to try and find Elijah. They thought that he had fallen in a valley.

And they said unto him, Behold now, there be with thy servants fifty strong men; let them go, we pray thee, and seek thy master, lest peradventure the Spirit of the LORD hath taken him up, and cast him upon some mountain, or into some valley. And he said, Ye shall not send. And when they urged him till he was ashamed, he said, Send. They sent therefore fifty men; and they sought three days, but found him not. (2 Kings 2:16, 17)

The sons of the prophets even convinced Elisha that he did not see what he actually saw. God wants to show us things in the Spirit realm.

Howbeit when he, the Spirit of truth, is come, he will guide you into all truth: for he shall not speak of himself; but whatsoever he shall hear, that shall he speak: and he will shew you things to come. (John 16:13)

Feast of Trumpets

Some people believe the next rapture occurs at the Feast of Trumpets. The seven feast do present prophetic implications. Let's look at the first four feast of Israel.

In the fourteenth day of the first month at even is the LORD'S passover. And on the fifteenth day of the same month is the feast of unleavened bread unto the LORD: seven days ye must eat unleavened bread. Speak unto the children of Israel, and say unto them, When ye be come into the land which I give unto you, and shall reap the harvest thereof, then ye shall bring a sheaf of the first fruits of your harvest unto the priest: Even unto the morrow after the seventh sabbath shall ye number fifty days; and ye shall offer a new meat offering unto the LORD. (Leviticus 23:5, 6,10,16)

Jesus fulfilled the first four feasts (Passover, Unleavened Bread, First Fruits and Pentecost). Jesus was the ultimate sacrifice at Passover.

126

Unleavened Bread represented Purity and Truth. Jesus is the Truth even while His body laid in a borrowed tomb during The Feast of Unleavened Bread. He was raised from the dead after the third day and **became the first fruits of them that slept** (1 Corinthians 15:20). Jesus ascended up into the clouds after preaching for forty days.

To whom also he shewed himself alive after his passion by many infallible proofs, being seen of them forty days, and speaking of the things pertaining to the kingdom of God. (Acts 1:3)

The disciples were told to tarry in Jerusalem until they received the Holy Ghost. The 120 people in The Upper Room heard the Holy Ghost come in like a mighty rushing wind. They all began to speak in other tongues as the Spirit of God gave them utterance (Acts 2:1-4). Seven days after Jesus was caught up in a cloud, the Holy Ghost was poured out. Jesus died at Passover and was raised up three days later. Jesus ministered for forty days after His resurrection. He ascended into the clouds forty three days from Passover. The Feast of Pentecost is exactly fifty days from Passover. So 43 from 50 leaves seven. Seven days after Jesus ascended back to heaven, the Holy Spirit filled 120 people and they began speaking in other tongues. Jesus created His church on the Day of Pentecost. The apostolic movement began as these disciples were filled with the power of God.

And there appeared unto them cloven tongues like as of fire, and it sat upon each of them. And they were all filled with the Holy Ghost, and began to speak with other tongues, as the Spirit gave them utterance. (Acts 2:1-4)

The next feast for Christ to fulfill is the Feast of Trumpets. I believe Jesus was born near this feast. He started his public ministry thirty years later, which fulfilled the law. Jesus prayed for people and they were healed

And Jesus himself began to be about thirty years of age. (Luke 3:23)

Paul said Christ would return at the sound of the last trump (1 Corinthians 15:52). A trumpet sounds an alarm or warning. In Thessalonians, Paul said the sound wakes up the dead.

The Lord Himself shall descend from heaven with a shout, with the voice of the archangel, and with the trump of God: and the dead in Christ shall rise first; Then we which are alive and remain shall be caught up together with them in the clouds to meet the Lord in the air: and so shall we ever be with the Lord.
(1 Thessalonians 4: 16, 17)

The Feast of Trumpets is called "The One Long Day" by the Jewish people. It now lasts for seventy two hours or three days. If Christ were to come on this feast, no one would know the day nor hour, because of the length of the feast. Jesus could return at the sound of this trumpet.

Speak unto the children of Israel, saying, In the seventh month, in the first day of the month, shall ye have a sabbath, a memorial of blowing of trumpets. (Leviticus 23:24)

What is F.E.M.A. Up To?

I have seen with my own eyes on video some of the facilities that F.E.M.A. (Federal Emergency Management Agency) has developed here in the United States. President Clinton gave F.E.M.A. the task of dividing America into ten regions in case of severe emergencies. If marshal law is needed, the Government has many facilities to keep people in. Anyone considered a threat by the government will be arrested. Facilities have been built to hold thousands of people such as gangs, militia groups, and anyone resisting government mandates. Left behind Christians will be put with these groups since they will be screaming for no one to accept a mark in their hand and forehead. The governments will be threatened by religious groups more than any other group. When unity occurs, no matter the cause, there is power in numbers.

Nuclear Weapons

When Jesus returns and destroys the armies at the battle of Armageddon, the earth will be in great distress. The sun will not shine and the moon will look like blood. This could be a picture of nuclear weapons or because of solar and lunar eclipses. If there are nuclear weapons exploding, then we can understand why Zechariah saw flesh melting on a man's body before he fell to the ground.

And this shall be the plague wherewith the Lord will smite all the people that have fought against Jerusalem; their flesh shall consume away while they stand upon their feet, and their eyes shall consume away in their holes, and their tongue shall consume away in their mouth. (Zechariah 14:12)

This seems to be a prophetic picture of nuclear warfare. Chernobyl in Russia is still melting and destroying soil and water tables. It is amazing that the word Chernobyl translated into Hebrew is Wormwood. John the Revelator spoke of a star called wormwood falling from heaven. It is not Chernobyl, but God was warning us of nuclear radiation that will occur in this world.

Chapter Eight

Generations in the Bible

Jesus is coming and this is the generation He is returning in. Now let's research the meaning of the word **generation,** and the years a generation consist of. I will explain three generations.

Verily I say unto you, this generation shall not pass, till all these things be fulfilled.
(Matthew 24:34)

God always warned His people ahead of time about tragedy and end time events. God is very precise and consistent in revealing future events. Biblical history is prophecy fulfilled. God gives us revelation about mysteries, numbers and names in the Bible to reveal his secret plans for mankind. Events are foretold for the past, present, and future. We will explore numbers and names to unveil God's plan for earth changing events.

Let's examine the meaning of some numbers first. One means unity, two means a witness, three represents the Godhead, four means praise, five means grace, six represents the number of man, seven means rest, and eight means a new beginning. Twelve equals governments, forty is testing, forty one means deliverance, and seventy represents leadership and righteousness. Three consecutive sixes represents the antichrist. Three consecutive eights represents the name of Jesus.

Forty Means Testing

I have skipped through these numbers to show an example. Let us look at the number forty. God caused it to rain for forty days and forty nights. Forty means testing or a wicked generation.

Surely there shall not one of these men of this evil generation see that good land which I swear to give unto your fathers. (Deuteronomy 1:35)

Forty years long was I grieved with this evil generation. (Deuteronomy 1:35)

Moses, Elijah, and Jesus fasted for forty days. Saul, David and Solomon ruled Israel forty years. Goliath taunted the children of Israel for forty days, but on the forty first day, David cut Goliath's head off. The number Forty is found again in scripture describing God's judgment.

Jonah cried, Yet forty days, and Nineveh shall be overthrown. (Jonah 3:4)

But the people of Nineveh were spared and delivered on the forty first day BECAUSE THEY

REPENTED. Jesus walked the earth forty days after His resurrection and preached the Word.

To whom also he shewed himself alive after his passion by many infallible proofs, being seen of them forty days, and speaking of the things pertaining to the kingdom of God. (Acts 1:3)

There are several more scriptures revealing a forty year generation in the Bible. (Deuteronomy 1:35, Psalms 95: 9,10; Hebrews 3:9,10). Israel became a sovereign nation on May 14, 1948. On May 14, 1989 Israel celebrated her 41st birthday. In 1989, Communism began to fall and over 250,000 Soviet Jews were released and allowed to go back to Israel. Forty one means deliverance.

Seventy Means Righteousness

Jeremiah warned Israel to turn back to God, or they were going into captivity for seventy years. The later part happened, and Israel was taken to Iraq for seventy years.

For thus saith the LORD, after seventy years be accomplished at Babylon I will visit you, and perform my good word toward you, in causing you to return to this place. (Jeremiah 29:10)

From 1919 (the year the Soviet Union became a

Marxist government) to 1989, fulfilled another seventy year period of captivity for the Jewish people.

Four Hundred Years

In the year 1917, the Jewish people were set free from the Turkish government by England after a four hundred year captivity.

And he said unto Abram, Know of a surety that thy seed shall be a stranger in a land that is not theirs, and shall serve them; and they shall afflict them four hundred years; But in the fourth generation they shall come hither again: for the iniquity of the Amorites is not yet full. (Genesis 15: 13, 16)

God told Abraham his people would experience 400 years of slavery, but after the fourth generation they would be delivered. Moses was used by God to deliver the people from Egypt. This proves that there is a one hundred year generation in the Bible (400 divided by 4 = 100). Some people think we have only been given seventy or eighty years, but God has promised us 120 years. If we ate right and exercised enough, we might live that long.

And the LORD said, My spirit shall not always strive with man, for that he also is flesh: yet his

days shall be an hundred and twenty years. (Genesis 6:3)

Events Before the Flood

Before the flood, man lived six, seven, eight, even nine hundred years. The oldest man in history according to the Bible reached 969 years. This man's name was Methuselah and he was Noah's grandfather. He died the same year the flood came. He may have warned people about the flood just by his name. **Methuselah's** name means - when he dies, then shall it come. Noah and his sons perhaps knew that Methuselah's name meant that, and they were watching him closely.

And all the days of Methuselah were nine hundred sixty and nine years: and he died. (Genesis 5:27)

Methuselah was 369 years old when Noah was born. Noah was 600 years old when the flood came. Methuselah was 969 years old when he died and the flood came. (Genesis 5:25-29; Genesis 7:6) In Genesis chapter 7, Shem's descendants had children near the age of thirty five years old. This is after the flood. The age of people producing children before the flood, were much older.

And Methuselah lived one hundred eighty and

135

seven years, and begat Lamech. And Lamech lived an hundred eighty and two years, and begat a son: And Noah was five hundred years old,and Noah begat Shem, Ham, and Japheth. (Genesis 5:25, 28, 32)

Before the flood, man lived to be very old. Methuselah was 969 years old when he died (Genesis 5:27). After the flood, man's length of years began to decrease. Man began producing new generations of children at an earlier age. Jesus said His return would be like the days of Noah.

But as the days of Noah were, so shall also the coming of the Son of man be. (Matthew 24:37)

People laughed at Noah building such a huge boat. Everyone was going about their business not taking heed to the warning Noah was giving them. People are doing that today. But there was something else going on that may have been over looked. I believe there was a lot of demonic activity taking place before and after the flood. We know that several fallen angels went into the daughters of men and produced giants in the land (Genesis 6:4,5). UFO'S were common in that day, just as they are common in our day. UFO'S are deception from fallen angels (Zachariah 5:5-11). Nimrod and all the people could not build a tower to heaven, because we can't do that even with all of

136

the best equipment. Nimrod was trying to build a landing base for UFO'S. He was deceived by these fallen angels and he wanted to communicate and obtain information from them. God stopped the construction. Remember that God said the people are one and nothing shall be restrained from them. Nimrod may have wanted to be worshiped, but God did not permit it.

The tower of Babel was in the land of Shinar, which is Iraq. Zachariah chapter five speaks of flying lead with a base in Shinar. Aircraft most of the time use a base. God said this is wickedness and this is their resemblance throughout all the earth. There has been so many UFO sightings and demonic activity going on that everyone accepts this as normal now. Fallen angels are trying to convince people that there is life on other planets and that God did not create man in His image, but this is deception.

Other Demonic Activity

Advocates for the New World Order (N.W.O.) presented evidence at a world forum held by Mikhail Gorbachev that usually three things cause war. These three things are political, economic and religious conflicts. Proposals were presented that wars would be prevented if there was a one world government, one world economy, and a one world religion. They said this would bring about peace and prosperity for the world. The bible says when the world speaks of peace and security then destruction is on the way.

For when they shall say, Peace and safety; then sudden destruction cometh upon them. (1 Thessalonians 5:3)

Office of the False Prophet

Destruction is surely on the way. Total peace on earth will only come when Jesus sits on a throne in Jerusalem. In these last days, the world will be governed and policed by the United Nations. The World is getting set for a cashless society. Laws were passed here in the USA that every new born child must have a social security number. The United Nations has now established a one world religious organization. It has representatives from every religion in the world. The UN is hoping and believing for a future Pope to be the leader of this one world religious organization. A Catholic Pope will one day make all religions worship the Antichrist. That specific Pope will be called the False Prophet. Remember, the false prophet's job is to convince everyone that the antichrist is God and everyone should worship him.

And causeth the earth and them that dwell

there in to worship. **(Revelation 13:12)**

Secret Societies

"Send us such a man and be he **god or devil,** we will receive him," said Paul Henri Spaak, first president of the United Nations. The world is being set up by world leaders to move us into the **New World Order.** There are some secret societies that want to rule the world and they have enormous influence and an unlimited bank account. They consist of The Illuminati, Freemasonry, Skull and Bones, The Bilderberg Group, Knights Templar, Trilateral Commission, and The Council on Foreign Affairs. Believe it or not, these groups have enormous power, money, influence and in many ways, they rule the world. I am patiently awaiting for my change to take place and I see Jesus face to face and I become just like Him.

Jewish Weddings

Something I would like to mention is the unique events of a Jewish wedding. It was a common practice in the Old Testament for a man to set a cup of wine at the door of his future bride. He would knock on the door and then back up. If the woman picks up the cup and drinks from it, she is saying that she will marry the groom. Jesus said we shall surely drink from the same cup He drank from. He was speaking of His Spirit living in us. We are a type of the bride and Jesus is a type of the bridegroom. The Jewish man will then go and build a home for them. He can take up to two years before he returns for the wedding. It has been two thousand years since Jesus left. He said in John 14 that He was going to prepare a place for us. After the wedding, the groom takes his bride away for seven days. He then brings her back and presents his bride to the community as his wife. Jesus will catch his bride up and keep us not seven days, but seven years. He then will bring us back with Him and we will enter the Millennial Reign.

Chapter Nine

The Meaning of Jacob's Trouble

Now let's go back to the number 490 times and the thought on forgiveness. I believe Jesus said for us to forgive 490 times because he knew that the Father's plan was to forgive mankind 490 years.

Seventy weeks are determined upon thy people and upon thy holy city, to finish the transgression, and to make an end of sin. (Daniel 9:24)

These seventy weeks mentioned are prophetic weeks. These weeks equal seven years each. Our weeks have seven days, but the Jewish prophetic week has seven years. Again we multiply seventy times seven (490 years). Here is a scripture that proves that a biblical prophetic week is seven years.

Fulfil her week, and we will give thee this also for the service which thou shalt serve with me yet seven other year. (Genesis 29:27)

Jacob had worked for seven years to get a wife, whom he thought would be Rachel. However, upon awakening on his honeymoon, he found Rachel's sister, Leah. Jacob's father in law told him to fulfill Rachel's week, and work for another seven years. The next seven years was hard for Jacob. He worked fourteen years to get the bride he wanted. The first seven years may not have been grievous to him, but the last seven had to be very tough. Jacob worked seven years and married Leah (by trickery from Laban). Then he worked seven years for Rachel. Jeremiah called the last part of the tribulation period Jacob's Trouble.

Alas! For that day is great, so that none is like it: it is even the time of Jacob's Trouble; but he shall be saved out of it. (Jeremiah 30:7)

And at that time shall Michael stand up, the great prince which standeth for the children of thy people: and there shall be a time of trouble, such as never was since there was a nation even to that same time; and at that time thy people shall be delivered, every one that shall be found written in the book. (Daniel 12: 1)

At the end of Daniel's seventieth week, the battle of Armageddon will take place. Many nations surround Jerusalem to make war against Israel. The Lamb of God shows up and stops their plan. One third of the Jewish people are saved and proclaim Jesus as the Messiah when He returns at the battle of Armageddon. Jesus then puts His feet on the Mount of Olives and proclaims a new day.

For I will gather all nations against Jerusalem to battle; and the city shall be taken, and the houses rifled, and the women ravished; and half of the city shall go forth into captivity, and the residue of the people shall not be cut off from the city. Then shall the LORD go forth, and fight against those nations, as when he fought in the day of battle. And his feet shall stand in that day upon. (Zechariah 14:2, 3, 4a)

The temple is cleansed and the earth is renewed. Christ will sit upon a throne in our sight for one thousand years. A leading Rabbi said the Ark of the Covenant was discovered in 1983 under the temple mount. However, they will not touch the ark until they have the ashes of a red heifer.

Jesus Sheds His Blood Seven Times

Since Jesus is a type of the red heifer, then He had to shed His blood seven times. Blood from the red heifer was sprinkled seven times (Numbers 19:4). Here are the seven times that Jesus shed His blood for the body of Christ.

1. He prayed so intense, that His sweat became as great drops of blood. (Luke 22:44)

2. The 39 stripes across His back with the leather whip (Matthew 27:26, I Peter 2:24). The Apostle

143

Paul said he received 40 strips, save one.

3. The crown of thorns upon His head. (Matthew 27:29)

4. They beat Him on His head, thus forcing the 3 inch thorns down into His scalp. (Matthew 27:30, Isaiah 53:2)

5. They pierced His hands with nails. (John 19: 18)

6. They drove a nail through His feet. (John 19: 18)

7. They pierced His side with a sword. (John 19:34)

Thank God for those precious stripes that Jesus received across His back. By His stripes we were healed! We can overcome the world if we walk with Jesus, because He has already overcome the world. Jesus has given us the faith and power to overcome any obstacle. We have the blood, the anointing, and the name of Jesus to win every battle. Greater is He that is in us, than He that is in the world.

Ask Jesus to Return

It's OK to ask Jesus to come back quickly.

And the Spirit and the bride say, Come. And let him that heareth say. Come. And let him that is a thirst come. And whosoever will, let him take the water of life freely. (Revelation 22:17)

The Word of God reveals that it is Biblical to ask for Jesus to return. I say come on Lord Jesus! I am ready to see my family that has gone on to heaven and I want to see Jesus. It will be neat to see the prophets of God all the way back to Adam. I also want a new glorified body.

Daniel's Seventy Weeks

Seventy weeks are determined upon thy people and upon the holy city, to finish the transgression, and to make an end of sins. Know therefore and understand, that from the going forth of the commandment to restore and to build Jerusalem unto the Messiah the Prince shall be seven weeks, and threescore and two weeks: and after threescore and two weeks shall Messiah be cut off, but not for himself: and the people of the prince that shall come shall destroy the city and the sanctuary. And he shall confirm the covenant with many for one week. (Daniel 9:24a, 25, 26, 27a)

The 490 year countdown started when the Jews were allowed to leave Iraq after seventy years of captivity. They went back and rebuilt Jerusalem and the temple. The seventy weeks of captivity were spoken by Jeremiah the prophet (Jeremiah 29:10). Daniel began to read Jeremiah's prophecy and realized that the 70 years were accomplished.

In the first year of his reign I Daniel understood by books the number of the years, whereof the word of the LORD came to Jeremiah the prophet, that he would accomplish seventy years in the desolations of Jerusalem. (Daniel 9:2)

The books of Ezra and Nehemiah give the account of God stirring up King Artaxerxes and King Cyrus of Babylon to make a decree to allow the Jews to go back to Jerusalem.

And it came to pass in the month Nisan, in the twentieth year of Artaxerxes the king, And I said unto the king, If it please the king, and if thy servant have found favor in thy sight, that thy wouldest send me unto Judah, unto the city of my father's sepulchres, that I may build it. (Nehemiah 2:1a, 5)

This FINAL DECREE to release the Jews had to be around the year 453 B.C. From this date until Jesus was crucified was exactly 69 weeks, or 483 years. Subtract 453 years from 483, and you have the time Jesus was crucified 29/30 A.D. It took seven weeks (49 years) to rebuild Jerusalem with 46 of these years rebuilding the temple.

Destroy this temple and in three days I will raise it up. Then said the Jews, Forty and six years was this temple in building, and wilt thou rear it up in three days? But he spake of the temple of his body. (John 2:19-21)

Let's now recap this information once more. It took 7 weeks (49 years) to complete the restoration of Jerusalem. From the year that Jerusalem was rebuilt to the crucifixion of Jesus was another 62 weeks (434 years). There is one week left to equal seventy weeks (7 weeks plus 62 weeks plus 1 week equals 70 weeks). The countdown stopped at the burial of Jesus Christ. Jesus did not die for Himself, but rather for mankind. The last week (7 years) will start when Israel signs a final peace treaty for seven years with her Arab neighbors (Daniel 9:24-27).

490 Years – A Prophetic Timetable

Luke 3:23 says Jesus started his public ministry at age thirty. The law required a priest to be thirty to fifty years old to be in the ministry (Numbers 4:47). It is believed that Jesus' public ministry lasted three and one half years. If we back up thirty three and one half years (the life of Christ) from the year 29/30 A.D., we are able to place the birth of Christ between 3 and 4 B.C. From the time Christ was crucified 29/30 A.D. to the year 1989 (the year the Soviet Jews were released), 4 different prophetic cycles (490 years each) elapsed. (29 A.D. plus 490 years = 519 A.D.); (519 AD plus 490 years = 1009 A.D.); (The year 1009 A.D. plus 490 years = 1499 A.D.); (The year 1499 A.D. plus 490 years = 1989 A.D.). Remember Luke 3:23-38 revealed four different 14 generations. This is why we've added 490 years four times. 490 years is a prophetic cycle; thus, the fourth prophetic cycle from Christ's crucifixion ended in 1989. No wonder at this time Jews began to speak about finding the Ark of the Covenant, the Ashes of the Red Heifer and the rebuilding of the temple. This is why Communism fell in Russia in 1989, and 250,000 Soviet Jews were allowed to go back to Israel. In fact, Jews from all over the world began moving back to Israel.

Some noted authors believe Christ was crucified around 33 A.D. For this to be correct, Jesus would have had to been born around 1 A.D. History tells us that Herod died around 2 B.C. There is also record of some type of comet at that same time. Remember the wise men saw a star, or something in the heavens in which they followed. Let's go back to the year 1989 again, and remember that

Jacob's Trouble originally was fourteen years (he worked 7 years for Leah and 7 years for Rachel). If we add fourteen years to 1989 we come to the year 2003. In 2003, the European Union (Revised Holy Roman Empire) finalized it's constitution and every country in the EU began using the Euro dollar. We went back to war with Iraq and removed Saddam Hussein. He fired 39 Scud missiles at Israel. God used the USA to take him out. In 1967, Israel fought and won the Six Day War. Jerusalem became the capital of Israel for the first time in 2,552 years.

And they shall fall by the edge of the sword, and shall be led away captive into all nations: and Jerusalem shall be trodden down of the Gentiles, until the times of the Gentiles be fulfilled. (Luke 21:24)

Gentiles (Arabs) lost some of their control over Jerusalem after the Six Day War. Some people think the rule of the Gentiles will be over when the first rapture takes place, but Gentiles will be here even to the very end. Gentiles will fight against Jesus at the end of the great tribulation. John the Revelator measured the new temple area, and revealed that Gentiles would control part of it.

Rise and measure the Temple of God and the altar and them that worship therein. But the

court which is without the temple leave out, and measure it not; for it is given unto the Gentiles: and the holy city shall they tread under foot forty and two months. (Revelation 11: 1, 2)

Scripture reveals that the Gentiles will have access to half the temple mount (Mount Moriah) for three and one half years. Eventually, the antichrist will set up his headquarters in Jerusalem. He will later destroy the holy city before Jesus returns. Ezekiel saw a vision of the third temple built in Jerusalem and he also saw a wall put up between the holy place and the profane.

Abraham did not offer Ishmael as the sacrifice in Genesis 22, he offered Isaac his promised son conceived by Sara. Ishmael was Abraham's first born, but he was not the promised son to be in the lineage of the Messiah. Ishmael produced the Arab population. There was another time the younger son received the blessing or inheritance over the elder brother. God told Rebekah that two nations were in her womb and the elder child would serve the younger (Genesis 25:23). God was referring to Esau serving Jacob.

The Six Day War

When looking back to the year 1967, not only did Israel recapture Jerusalem and make it the capital, but it happened to be exactly fifty years after coming out of the four hundred year captivity of the Turkish government (1917 to 1967 = 50 years); (1517 to 1917 = 400 years). Israel signed the Balfour Estate with England in 1917 after General Allenby helped deliver Israel from the Turkish government. The number fifty represents freedom, joy and jubilee.

And ye shall hallow the fiftieth year, and proclaim liberty throughout all the land unto all the inhabitants thereof; it shall be a jubilee unto you, and ye shall return every man unto his possession, and ye shall return every man unto his family. (Leviticus 25:10)

In the Year of the Jubilee, slaves were released, land was returned and debts were forgiven. In 1967, Jerusalem was returned to Israel after the Six Day War. On the seventh day, Israel was marching through the same land that Joshua and the children of Israel marched through after the fall of the walls of Jericho. Joshua led Israel around the walls six days. On the seventh day, Joshua marched through Jericho, the Gaza strip and the Golan Heights.

Vision of the Year 2003

If we add the generation of a Jewish man which is 35 **full** years to the end of 1967, we come to year 2003. We maybe on borrowed time ever since 2003. The Lord gave me a vision in 1986. I saw a cloud appear in the ceiling with the appearance of the Lord standing in the middle of the cloud. Beside his left shoulder was the number 2003. I was fully awake, because I had been studying the Word of God. I studied the vision, as it lasted for about forty five seconds. I asked Jesus what the vision meant, but he assured me that I would understand in due time. Then in May of 1989, God revealed to me that the vision represented the year 2003. He later revealed that the United States would go to war against Iraq. He did say He was pouring His spirit out worldwide starting in this selfsame month and year (May 1989). Prophecy in the Word of God began to be illuminated right before my eyes. By understanding the past and future events, they began to line up and fit like a puzzle. Jesus began to put the thought in my spirit of working while it is day. The harvest is now more than ever.

I must work the works of Him that sent me, while it is day: the night cometh, when no man can work. (John 9:4)

Be patient therefore, brethren, unto the coming of the Lord. Behold, the husbandman waiteth for the precious fruit of the earth, and hath long patience for it, until he receive the early and

latter rain. Be ye also patient; establish your hearts: for the coming of the Lord draweth nigh. (James 5:7,8)

A latter rain (another wave of Glory) began in May of 1989. From 1989 to 2003 is 14 years or two 7 year cycles. Remember Jacob and Joseph both dwelt with 14 year cycles. A time of harvest is now and the latter rain is here. As we lift up Jesus, He will draw all men unto Him. Joseph, which was one of Jacob's twelve sons often received dreams and visions about the future. He later told Pharaoh to prepare for 7 years of harvest and then 7 years of famine.

Behold there come seven years of great plenty throughout all the land of Egypt: and there shall arise after them seven years of famine. (Genesis 41:29, 30a)

Egypt represented the world and the harvest of plenty can represent souls for the kingdom of God. The famine represents Daniel's 70th week. Israel signed a seven year covenant with the PLO in 1993 which expired in the year 2000. Negotiations are ongoing for the next seven year treaty.

The Pope and the False Prophet

The Apostle Paul said in II Thessalonians 2 that

the man of sin (the Antichrist) would proclaim himself as God. Israel and the world will receive the false messiah at first but will realize the Antichrist is not the prophesied messiah as he breaks the seven year treaty. The False Prophet (the most well known religious figure on earth) will proclaim this false messiah as God. As the False Prophet pulls back the veil in the temple and reveals the man of sin, Israel will see a statue or image behind the veil. The Antichrist will have power to make the image move and speak (Revelation 13:15). Only at this time will Israel denounce this false messiah. He will then begin another holocaust of the Jewish people (Zechariah 13:8). A third of the Jewish people will escape the great tribulation period and receive Jesus as their Messiah. The nation of Jordan will become a close friend to Israel during the tribulation period.

The Fourth Kingdom

When the Jewish people flee after seeing the statue in the temple, they will hide in an area of Jordan called Petra. Petra means the rock. We that are born again by the blood of Jesus recognize that Christ Jesus is our Rock. He is the Rock of Ages, the Chief Cornerstone of our faith. In Daniel 7:23, a fourth kingdom is mentioned that will devour the Earth. The fourth kingdom will be ruled by the Antichrist. There have been several men who could fill the role of the first 3 antichrists. These men have tried to rule the world and destroy Israel. Alexander the Great, Napoleon, and Hitler tried this in times past. Hitler's regime was called the Third Reich. Some Scholars have put Nero and Antiochus Epiphanes in the place of Alexander and Napoleon. Daniel saw the forth Reich or kingdom more diverse than all the rest. This fourth beast will be the Little Horn or a man possessed with Satan himself. His time is close because the temple is close to being rebuilt. A man named Gershon Solomon has founded an organization (The Temple Mount Faithful) to rebuild the temple very soon.

A Day of Rest is Coming

Howbeit when He, the Spirit of Truth, is come, He will guide you into all truth: for He shall not speak of Himself; but whatsoever He shall hear, that shall He speak: and He will show you things to come. (John 16:13)

God wants to reveal mysteries to His people. Although the Lord will never reveal the day nor hour of His Return, we are able to discern the signs of the times. The Millennial Reign shall be a time of rest for the people of God. Although we will have jobs to do for Jesus, we will not get tired.

For He spake in a certain place of the seventh

day on this wise and God did rest the seventh day from all His works. Seeing therefore it remaineth that some must enter therein, and they to whom it was first preached entered not in because of unbelief. There remaineth therefore a rest to the people of God. (Hebrews 4: 4, 6, 9)

If we endure to the end and remain faithful to God, we not only receive great rewards and a new body, but we will also receive a new name.

But he that shall endure to the end, the same shall be saved. (Matthew 24: 13)

To him that overcometh will I give to eat of the hidden Manna, and will give him a white stone, and in the stone a new name written, which no man knoweth saving him that receiveth it. (Revelation 2: 17b)

Even Jesus will have a new name that no man knows.

And He had a name written, that no man knew, but He himself. (Revelation 19: 12b)

We will rule the nations with Christ Jesus as kings and priests here on Earth with new names, Praise the Lord!.

156

And he that overcometh, and keepeth my works unto the end, to him will I give power over the nations: And he shall rule them with a rod of iron. (Revelation 2:26,27)

A time of rest is promised to us for working for the kingdom of God.

Six Days or 6,000 Years

Many notable scholars have believed that the six thousandth year or sixth day would end the dispensation of grace and usher in the Millennial Reign. I have compared six thousand years with six days just as Peter did.

But, beloved, be not ignorant of this one thing, that one day is with the Lord as a thousand years, and a thousand years as one day. (II Peter 3:8)

The Word of God is forever settled and cannot change. In understanding the future, one must only look at the past. God created everything in six days with woman being the last thing He created. Then on the seventh day, God rested (Genesis 2:2). He was establishing an order for man to follow. We work six days and then rest on the seventh. Man must till the Earth for six thousand years and then he can rest for a thousand years in a new body.

And God said, Let us make man in our image, after our likeness. (Genesis 1:26)

And God saw everything that He had made, and behold, it was very good. And the evening and the morning were the sixth day. (Genesis 1:31)

Peter said one day with the Lord is like a thousand years to mankind. A thousand years to mankind is like one day with the Lord. From Adam to Abraham was two thousand years, or two days. From Abraham to Christ was two thousand years, or two days. From the birth of Christ (between 4 B.C. and 3 B.C.) until now is two thousand years, or two days. This totals six days.

After two days will He revive us: in the third day He will raise us up, and we shall live in his sight. (Hosea 6:2)

Man is about to be raised up to meet the Lord in the air. Man was made on the sixth day and raised up to walk and talk with God. I believe we are going to be raised up very soon. We shall live in the presence of the Lord and rest for one day or a thousand years. At the end of the Millennial Reign, or third day from the birth of Christ, we will enter the seventh day. John 2:1 reveals Jesus at a marriage feast on the third day. Verse six of this same chapter says Jesus called for the six water pots used to purify the Jews. It is interesting to think of Jesus using 6000 years (six water pots) to purify mankind. Jesus turned the water into wine in verse nine. The governor of the feast was amazed that the wine tasted better than the wine that was set out at the beginning. The wine represents the anointing of God. Jesus wants us to know that the anointing will be greater and stronger and more plentiful here at the end of this last dispensation than it has ever been before. The Governor in John 2:10 said the latter wine was better than the former. The anointing is greater in these last days than ever before. As sin increases, the grace of God is also increasing (Romans 5:20).

Warning Signs

People are looking for signs to warn them before Jesus comes back. People want to live much to close to the edge. The Pharisees ask Jesus for a sign from heaven not realizing that He was the sign from heaven.

Oh ye hypocrites, ye can discern the face of the sky; but can ye not discern the signs of the times? A wicked and adulterous generation seeketh after a sign; and there shall no sign be given unto it, but the sign of the prophet Jonas. And he left them and departed. (Matt. 16:3,4)

The Spirit of the Lord is speaking to his people through his prophets again. The prophets of the Lord have gone their own way but now are arising to warn Nineveh (the world) that things are going to happen in so many days. A cry began in 1988 throughout America with a book called, *88 Reasons Why the Rapture Will Be in 1988*. Many people are serving God today because of that warning. The author of that book made a terrible mistake in choosing a certain date for Jesus to return (September 13, 1988). We will never know the day nor hour of Christ's return.

The signs of Jonah also included him sitting under the shade tree resting, rather than warning people to repent. Many people today have become a sign of the prophet Jonah. Whether we see anything take place or not, more warnings will be given. A generation of people will hear and repent, just as the days of Nineveh, when 120,000 people came to the Lord. There are multitudes of people that are in trouble spiritually, physically, and emotionally, but we have an answer. Jesus can bring them out victoriously!

The Peace Treaty Of 1993

I have some more information about the peace treaty of 1993. In September of 1993, the Palestine Liberation Organization, or PLO, and the Israeli government signed a document to begin a peace process. This would also put in motion for the PLO to govern themselves and for the Israeli forces to withdraw from the occupied territories. This document is called the "Doctrine of Principles." This could initiate a covenant or peace treaty between Israel and her Arab neighbors in our generation. The Foreign Minister of Israel at that time, Shimon Perez, also signed the document on the White House lawn. This document was not the **covenant** being confirmed by the Antichrist, nor did the signing of this document start Daniel's 70th week, but it is the forerunner. I HAVE A COPY OF THIS DOCUMENT ON PAGE 175. Eventually a peace treaty will be confirmed and Shimon Perez may be involved because his name means a broken covenant. The name Perez (spelled three ways, Pharez, Perez and Peres), means a breach.

And it came to pass, as he drew back his hand, that behold, his brother came out: and she said, How has thou broken forth? This breach be upon thee: therefore his name was called Pharez. (Genesis 38:29)

Judah had gone into his daughter in law Tamar, and did not know it was her. She conceived and had twins. The child to break forth first withdrew and the next child came out. The handmaiden named him Pharez because Pharez means a broken agreement. The second time the name Pharez is used is found in II Samuel.

And the anger of the Lord was kindled against Uzzah; and God smote him there for his error; and there he died by the ark of God. And David was displeased, because the Lord had made a breach upon Uzzah: and he called the name of the place Perez-Uzzah to this day. (II Samuel 6:7, 8)

Shimon Perez may be involved in the signing of Daniel's 70th week, but I'm not saying he is the Antichrist. God uses names and numbers to fulfill events, and warn his people. Yitzak Rabin, the late Prime Minister of Israel is also a warning because of the meaning of his name. The word <u>many</u> is derived from the Hebrew root word *rav* or *rab* and also translates ravin or Rabin. It means great or multitude. From this root word comes the familiar word rabbi. The word <u>many</u> may represent a certain leader of Israel or perhaps a group of leaders of Israel. Yitzak Rabin got the peace process started before he was assassinated. Scripture does not say that the Antichrist will make up a covenant or agreement, but rather, he will strengthen one already in existence. The Antichrist will only honor this "covenant" he confirms or strengthens for half of the seven years. <u>Confirm</u> used as a verb, means to strengthen, make strong, or acknowledge. The Antichrist will **confirm the covenant with many for one week (Daniel 9:27).**

Jesus will return at the end of the tribulation period and have Satan chained up. This will be the day of the Lord. When we see the words **"The day of the Lord,"** it refers to the Lord returning at the end of the tribulation.

Behold, the day of the Lord cometh, and thy spoil shall be divided in the midst of thee. For I will gather all nations against Jerusalem to battle. (Zechariah 14:1, 2a)

Disasters In the USA

The U.S. should never force Israel to trade land for peace. Every time we put pressure on Israel to trade land, we end up losing property. Here is proof that disasters happen to the USA when we force Israel to give up land. These disasters don't even include Hurricane Katrina and the massive oil spill in May of 2010.

1. October 30, 1991

The Perfect Storm - President George W. Bush began a Conference in Spain to consider "land for peace" in Israel. At the same time, a storm hit the North Atlantic with 35 foot waves that eventually hit the home of President Bush.

2. August 23, 1992

Hurricane Andrew - The Madrid Peace Conference moved to Washington, DC and the peace talks resumed. Hurricane Andrew (which was the worst natural disaster in America up to that time),came ashore and produced an estimated $30 billion in damage and left 180,000 homeless in Florida.

3. January 16, 1994

California Earthquake - President Clinton met with Syria's President Assad and talked about Israel giving up the Golan Heights. Within 24 hours, a 6.9 earthquake rocked Southern California. This earthquake was the 2nd worst natural disaster to hit the U.S. up to that time.

4. January 21, 1998

Monica Lewinsky Scandal - Israeli Prime Minister Benjamin Netanyahu is scheduled to meet with President Clinton in Washington, DC but is turned down. Within hours, the Monica Lewinsky scandal was introduced by the news media and began to occupy most of Clinton's presidency.

5. September 28, 1998

Hurricane George - Secretary of State Albright finished an agreement that would cause Israel to give up 13 percent of (Judah and Samaria). Hurricane George slammed into the US Gulf Coast with wind gusts up to 175 mph. Arafat later spoke to the UN demanding a Palestinian state. Hurricane George caused one billion in damages. When Arafat departed the US, the storm calmed down.

6. October 15-22, 1998

Texas Flooded - On October 15, 1998, Arafat and Netanyahu meet in Maryland. The talks are scheduled to last five days with the focus on Israel giving up 13 percent of their land. Two days later, awesome rains and tornadoes hit southern Texas. The rain and flooding in Texas continue until October 22. The floods ravaged 25 percent of Texas and cause one billion dollars in damage.

7. November 30, 1998

Market Capitalization Evaporates - Arafat comes to Washington, DC again to meet with President Clinton to raise money for a Palestinian state with Jerusalem as the capital. Clinton promised $400 million in aid. On the same day, the Dow Jones drops 216 points, and the next day the European Market had its third worst day in history. Billions were wiped out in the US and Europe.

8. December 12, 1998

Clinton is Impeached – Clinton lands in Tel Aviv and then travels to the Palestinian controlled section of Israel. As he begins to discuss the "land for peace" deal, the House of Representatives votes four articles of impeachment against him.

9. May 3, 1999

Super Tornado - The very day that Yasser Arafat was scheduled to declare a Palestinian state with Jerusalem as the capital, the most powerful tornado storm system ever to hit the United States sweeps across Oklahoma and Kansas. The winds are clocked at 316 mph, the fastest wind speed ever recorded. Arafat's declaration is postponed to December 1999 at the request of President Clinton, which later wrote that the Palestinians have a right to "determine their own future on their own land."

The last one I want to mention actually started as over 250,000 Jews were about to leave Russia. Our government thought they should tell Israel to make settlers move to satisfy the Palestinians.

10. October 1989

Hurricane, Earthquake and Dow Collapse - As Jewish settlers in 15 Israel settlements are evicted from the covenant land in Israel, the Dow Jones financial averages lose 5.7 percent in the worst week since October 1989. On October 15 the Dow lost 266 points, and a hurricane slams into North Carolina. The next morning, a magnitude 7.1 earthquake rocked the southwest in the fifth most powerful earthquake in the 20th Century. The earthquake was felt in three states.

Chapter Ten

Nineteen Year Cycles

I was awakened by the Holy Spirit in October of 2007 at 4:30 am. The Lord told me to get up and write down some unique information concerning 19 year cycles. I had heard of many cycles such as 7 weeks, 7 years, 40 years, 490 years, etc...but not 19 years. I was very sleepy and complaining to the Lord to tell me later. He won the battle and I got up and began to write down what He said. The Lord showed me several periods that were all 19 years each. The number 19 means **Divine order and can be connected with judgment.**

The Lord revealed to me what prophetic events occurred at the beginning and end of these 19 year cycles. Some cycles were in consecutive order while others were not. A few of these cycles dealt with events in my own life, while the rest were world events. I will explain a few of these cycles in detail. The Lord began with the year 1900 and then spoke 1919. Then I heard the years: 1919 to 1938, then 1938 to 1957, then 1917 to 1936, then 1948 to 1967, then 1967 to 1986), and finally 1993 to 2012. I will begin with the year **1900**. At the turn of the 19 century, the Zionist movement began as a group of Jewish people sought to repurchase land in Israel to rebuild their homeland. During the same time, there was a worldwide outpouring of the Holy Spirit. In **1919,** Russia became a Marxist government and began conquering most of Europe. Thousands of Jews had began to travel throughout Europe and unknowingly, were trapped in the future USSR. From this date however, just 70 years later, 250,000 Jews would leave Russia and go back to Israel. This Exodus would fulfill another part of Jeremiah 29:10,14.

The next nineteen year cycle is **1938.** This was the year that Hitler began to put Jews into concentration camps. Six million Jews were killed, but eventually six million Germans were also killed during World War II. Ezekiel 38:11 God revealed that the Jewish people would become a valley of dry bones (Holocaust). However, God makes them a nation just a few years later.

The next nineteen year prophetic cycle is in the year **1957.** The treaty of Rome is signed, thus beginning the rebirth of the old Roman Empire. The European Community desired to bring all of Europe under one umbrella. Germany had to become one country for this to work and it happened in 1989. Revelation 13 explains the ten kings coming to power with the Antichrist. The EU IS JUST ONE OF THESE KINGS. Keep an eye on the G-8. They are the richest industrialized nations in the world. This group could become the G-10 and they also could fit the bill of the ten kings spoken of in Daniel 7:24 and Revelation 17:12.

Lets go back for a moment and pick up events in 1917 and 1936. In **1917**, Israel signed the Balfour Treaty with England. This broke the four hundred year captivity that the Turkish government held over Israel. This started the march for Israel to become a nation again. In **1936,** the rise of Hitler and his march to rule the world and destroy the Jewish people was prophetic. Hitler called his regime the Third Reich. Daniel 7:17 reveals four world leaders, with the fourth being the Antichrist. For Hitler to be the third evil ruler, we now know we are close to Jesus' return.

1948 was the year Israel became a nation, thus fulfilling Ezekiel 37:21,22. Just nineteen years later in **1967**, Israel recaptures Jerusalem in the Six Day War. It had been over 2500 years since Jerusalem was the capital of Israel. As the fig tree begins to bloom, another Holy Spirit outpouring begins with the Charismatic movement. Many denominations experienced Pentecost and millions of Christians became intercessory prayer warriors. On a personal note, nineteen years later in **1986,** Jesus raised me up out of a twenty seven day brain dead coma. I have been given a second chance to feed the body of Christ, and warn everyone that Jesus is real and He is coming soon. I am just a messenger along with millions more that is looking for that great day when we see Jesus face to face. I can not cover every nineteen year cycle God gave me in this section, but I will share one more with you. The last nineteen year cycle that the Holy Spirit gave me was 1993 to 2012. In the year of **1993,** the European Community eventually was created by the Maastricht Treaty and came into force in November 1993. Home computers were becoming increasingly common paving the way for the Internet and instant global communication.

The greatest prophetic event of 1993 was Israel signing a seven year treaty with the Palestinians. The treaty expired in September of 2000, but another seven year treaty will soon be signed. Also in 1993, the top Orthodox Jews developed, adopted, and signed a new document establishing a promise to protect Jerusalem. This became known as (The Jerusalem Covenant Document). I have enclosed a copy of this document on page 175.

Closing Thoughts About 2012

Nineteen years after the historic treaty of 1993 is the year **2012**. Much has already been said about the sun, moon, and stars in previous chapters. Scientists and astrologists all agree that the Sun will be reaching it's 11TH year peak called **solar maximum** at the end of 2012. The last solar blast occurred on November 4, 2003. The world will not end in 2012, but there could be world changing events. The sun could knock out several communication satellites which could make us vulnerable to terrorist attacks. These solar blast could also overload power grids, causing massive blackouts. There is a lot of debate about polar shifts that occur on the sun and the earth. If earthquakes get any worse than what we have witnessed already in 2010, it will get real ugly. Remember the Obama health care program (if it does not change), could force Americans to receive medical implants. The U.S. presidential election in in 2012 will be very prophetic within itself. However, I believe the election of the new Secretary General of the United Nations in 2012 is even more prophetic.

Also remember that the number nineteen means divine order and can be connected to judgment. If Obama or the next president forces Israel to divide Jerusalem with the Palestinians, then America will also be divided, either by an earthquake, economic disaster or a political race war. If people will repent, seek God's face, and keep all of His commandments, He will heal our land and hold back His judgment. However, we all know that people will get more wicked and gross darkness will cover the world. God will be forced to pour out His judgment, because His Word says so. I

171

would suggest that we serve the Lord Jesus with all of our heart and love one another. If we will forgive each other and walk in peace and holiness, we will be just fine. It does not matter when Jesus returns as long as we are ready. It does not matter how bad things get as long as we remember Jesus said He will never leave us. Become a bold disciple for Jesus today and witness to everyone you meet. You may be the only person others will listen to. You might just be the key to your entire family receiving Christ. If this little book helps one person get saved and go to heaven, it is worth every dollar spent, the long nights without sleep, and countless hours of study.

You might not agree with me 100 percent on every thing I have written in this book, but that is OK, I have never met anyone that I agree 100 percent with on everything either. I look forward to spending eternity in heaven with you and your family. The next few pages are amazing documents that few people have seen. They are priceless in revealing the time in which we live. May God's favor always shine upon you,

Your friend in Jesus,
International Evangelist Richard L. Madison

Please consider helping us put this book in every person's hand. You may order a case of these books at half price.

Chapter Eleven

The Covenant of Jerusalem

On May 19,1993, a document called the Covenant of Jerusalem was affirmed by seventy prominent Jewish leaders around the world. Over 1,500 people of the Israeli government were on hand for the signing of this document. God used seventy men to help Moses lead the Hebrews.

And the Lord said unto Moses, Gather unto me seventy men of the elders of Israel, whom thou knowest to be the elders of the people. (Numbers 11: 16a)

A council of seventy men called the Sanhedrin recently were used to discuss important questions concerning the nation of Israel. This seventy man council carried over from Moses to the New Testament. While the people of Israel search for peace, scripture declares there will be no peace until Jesus sets up his Millennial Kingdom.

To wit, the prophets of Israel which prophesy concerning Jerusalem, and which see vision of peace for her, and there is no peace, saith the Lord. (Ezekiel 13:16)

For when they shall say, Peace and Safety; then

sudden destruction cometh upon them, as travail upon a woman with child; and they shall not escape. (2 Thessalonians 5:3)

Strengthen ye the weak hands and confirm the feeble knees. Say to them that are of a fearful heart. Be strong, fear not: behold, God will come with vengeance, Even God with a recompense; He will come and save you. Then the eyes of the blind shall be opened and the ears of the deaf shall be unstopped. Then shall the lame man leap as a hart and the tongue of the dumb sing and a highway shall be there, and a way, and it shall be called the Way of Holiness, the unclean shall not pass over it. No lion shall be there, nor any ravenous beast shall go up thereon, it shall not be found there; but the redeemed shall walk there. (Isaiah 35:3-9)

There is coming a day when there will not be anyone blind, halt or withered. You will not see policemen, ambulances, or hospital staffs helping to revive people from disasters. That is going to be a great day!

The Jerusalem Covenant Document

As of this day, Jerusalem Day, the twenty eighth day of the month of Iyar in the year five thousand seven hundred fifty two; one thousand nine hundred and twenty two years after the destruction of the Second Temple; forty four years since the founding of the State of Israel; twenty five years since the Six Day War during which the Israel Defense Forces, in defense of our very existence, broke through the walls of the city and restored the Temple Mount and the unity of Jerusalem; twelve years since the Knesset of Israel reestablished that Jerusalem, unified and whole, is the Capital of Israel; the State of Israel is the State of the Jewish People and the Capital of Israel is the Capital of the People in Israel.

We have gathered together in Zion, national leaders and heads of our great communities everywhere, to enter into covenant with Jerusalem, as was done by the leaders of our nation and all the people of Israel upon Israel's return to its Land from the Babylonian exile; and the people and their leaders vowed to dwell in Jerusalem, the Holy City. Jerusalem built as a city joined together which unites the people of Israel to one another, and links heavenly Jerusalem with this earthly Jerusalem. We have returned to the place that the

Lord vowed to bestow upon the descendants of
Abraham, Father of our Nation; to the City of
David, King of Israel; where Solomon, son of
David, built a Holy Temple; a Capital City which
became the Mother of all Israel; a metropolis for
justice and righteousness and for the wisdom and
insights of the ancient world; where a Second
Temple was erected in the days of Ezra and
Nehemiah. In this city the prophets of the Lord
prophesied; in this City the Sages taught Torah; in
this City the Sanhedrin convened in session in its
stone chamber. For there were the seats of Justice,
the Throne of the House of David, for out of Zion
shall go forth Torah, and the Word of the Lord
from Jerusalem.

Today, as of old, we hold fast to the truth of the
words of the Prophets of Israel, that all the
inhabitants of the world shall enter within the gates
of Jerusalem: And it shall come to pass at the end
of days, the mountain of the House of the Lord
will be well established at the peak of the
mountains and will tower above the hills, and all
the nations shall stream towards it. Each and every
nation will live in it by its own faith: For all the
nations will go forward, each with its own Divine
Name; we shall go in the name of the Lord our
God forever and ever. And in this spirit the Knesset
of the State of Israel has enacted a law: the places
holy to the peoples of all religions shall be

protected from any desecration and from any restriction of free access to them. Jerusalem - peace and tranquility shall reign in the city: Pray for the peace of Jerusalem; may those who love you be tranquil. May there be peace within your walls, and tranquility within your palaces. Out of Jerusalem, a message of peace went forth and shall yet go forth again to all the inhabitants of the earth:

In the future, The Holy One, the Blessed, will comfort Jerusalem only with peace in this place, we once again take this vow: If I forget thee, 0 Jerusalem, may my right hand lose its strength; may my tongue cleave to my palate if I do not remember you, if I do not raise up Jerusalem at the very height of my rejoicing. And with all these understandings, we enter into this Covenant and write: We shall bind you to us forever; and we shall bind you to us with faithfulness, with righteousness and justice, with steadfast love and compassion.

We love you, O Jerusalem, with eternal love, with unbounded love, under siege and when liberated from the yoke of oppressors. We have been martyred for you; we have yearned for you, we have clung to you. Our faithfulness to you as we shall bequeath to our children after us. Forevermore, our home shall be within you.

Prayer to be Born Again

Father, I come to You in the name of Your son, Jesus Christ, confessing with my mouth and believing in my heart according to Your Word in Romans 10:9 that Jesus died for my sins and was dead three days. I am a sinner and I have fallen short of the glory of God and I repent of all my sins. Come into my heart and life right now and save me. I believe Jesus was raised from the dead and now He lives in me. I am now born again and a new creature in Christ Jesus. I will be baptized in water and I shall receive the gift of the Holy Ghost. I proclaim the precious blood of Jesus over my soul and I am saved. I will testify that Jesus is Lord of Lords and King of Kings forever in my life. I will pray and seek your face everyday and draw close to You. Thank You for writing my name in the Lamb's Book of Life. I am redeemed from the curse of the law and the sin of death. I now have eternal life because I believe.

Amen.

RAISED from the DEAD
A TRUE ACCOUNT
by Richard L. Madison

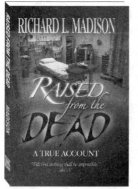

Following a horrible car accident, Richard Madison was rushed to the hospital and pronounced dead on arrival. His family was told three times to make funeral arrangements. God raised Richard up out of a brain dead coma and ten weeks later he walked out of a wheelchair.

He is now a walking miracle testimony to thousands of people throughout the world that God's love can powerfully restore even the most hopeless lives. As you read this true story you will discover how you can...

- Hear directly from God
- Know God's will and purpose for your life
- Defeat Satan's power over you
- Operate in the gifts of the Spirit
- Prosper as God watches over your finances
- Receive physical healing
- Minister healing to others

$15.00 includes US shipping
ISBN: 9780942507430

Case of **40 Books** - $7.50 each, includes S/H on US orders.

LEVANTADO de la MUERTE

por Richard L. Madison

Rick Madison era ingresado cadáver, pero por milagro de Dios fue revivido!

"Richard, usted es un milagro vivo; ciertamente hay un Dios del cielo que está velando por usted."—Dr. Kenneth Sharp, Hospital de la Universidad de Vanderbilt

"Richard fue resucitado de la muerte a fin de ayudar a miles a ser salvados y sanados. Profetizó eventos del mundo antes de que hubieran ocurrido, por ejemplo, los terremotos, las guerras en Iraq, y los ataques del 11 de septiembre."—Sid Roth, Fundador y Presentador del programa de televisión "It's Supernatural"

• Oír directamente de Dios
• Conocer la voluntad y el propósito de Dios para su vida
• Operar en los dones del Espíritu
• Prosperar mientras Dios cuida de sus finanzas
• Recibir sanidad física
• Ministrar sandidad a otros

Richard Madison es un evan-gelista a tiempo completo, quien viaja alrededor del mundo para decir la notable historia de cómo Dios le levanto de su lecho de muerte y completamente lo libró de las drogas y el alcohol. Richard es un orador muy buscado con un poderoso ministerio de sanidad y profecía. El y su familia viven en Oakman, AL

$15.00 includes US Shipping
ISBN 978-0942507447

END TIME PROPHECY REVEALED
By Richard L. Madison

One of the most powerful and informative books ever written about end time events. Learn the secrets of Daniel's 70 weeks, the event that begins the last seven years known as the tribulation period. Also includes information on the United Nations, the Antichrist, the banking industry, U.S. Presidents, and Earth's new ten divisions that will usher in the new world order.

God revealed to Rev. Madison several earthquakes, the 9/11 attack, and the wars with Iraq before they occurred. This book reveals prophetic cycles of 2012, Israel's next war, and the third temple. Discover the 8 raptures from Enoch to the White Throne Judgment linked to the first 8 letters of the Hebrew alphabet.

Discover the recent birth of red heifers in Israel, and the development of the microchip implants. Richard reveals the two witnesses, the false prophet, and the generation Jesus returns in. Also included is the Jerusalem Covenant Document signed in 1993. This book is a must for anyone interested in eschatology and future prophetic events. We are living in the last days and this book proves it. A great book to give to your unsaved family and friends.

$15.00 includes US shipping
ISBN 9780578044231

Case of **40 Books** - $7.50 each, includes S/H on US orders.

THE ANOINTING, POWER, & GIFTS OF GOD

By Richard L. Madison

Discover what it means to be born again and how to receive power through the infilling of the Holy Spirit. Learn how to hear the voice of God and be led by His Spirit.

The Anointing, Power, and Gifts of God will reveal the Biblical truths about salvation, water baptism, and the baptism of the Holy Ghost. Learn about the gifts of the Spirit, how they operate, and how to flow in them. Uncovered are seven purposes of the Holy Ghost, and what the Bible reveals is the evidence of being filled with the Holy Spirit.

Learn about the fruit of the Spirit and how to apply them to your life. This is a biblical tool that helps explain the anointing of God, receiving revelation knowledge and how to have a personal relationship with Jesus Christ. This book will cause a spiritual river to start flowing out of you.

Find out how to be a bold witness and win souls to the Kingdom of God. This is a perfect book to share with others about the Holy Spirit and living in total victory.

$15.00 includes US shipping
ISBN 9780578037363

Case of **40 Books** - $7.50 each, includes S/H on US orders.

Ministry DVDs

1.End Time Prophecy Vol. 1
This DVD covers the year 2012, prophetic cycles, signs of Jesus' return, US Presidents and Daniel's Seventy weeks. 2nd message titled Mystery of the Hours. It also covers the last days and how soon Jesus is coming back.. (2 hrs)

2.End Time Prophecy Vol. 2
Two powerful messages unlike any you may have ever heard. The 1st message is The Lion, Bear, and the Serpent. The 2nd hour is Satan's Three Missing Stones. I promise this series will take you to another level. (2 hrs)

3.Raised from the Dead - Rick's Miracle Testimony
Richard shares his Miracle Testimony during a church service. The second message is titled Ashes of the Red Heifer and includes a powerful healing service. (2 hrs)

4.Interview with Sid Roth / Anointing & Funny Stories
This DVD includes 4 TV programs - It's Supernatural with Sid Roth (actors re-enacting Richard's testimony). Richard appears on Daystar with Marcus and Joni Lamb. The 3rd message is on the Anointing. Part 4 includes true funny stories that has occurred in Rick's services. (2 hrs)

5.The Faith and Miracle DVD Series
Richard shares on how to use your faith and receive from God. This includes miracles that Richard has seen such as 20 coma patients waking up, people walking out of several wheelchairs. You will learn how to pray for the sick and believe for the supernatural. (2 hrs)

6.Entertaining Angels and Seeing in the Spirit- 2 power packed messages that includes Richard sharing his encounters with real angels. Richard then shares on the lives of Elijah and Elisha and how they are a type of the end times. Richard also shares on how to see in the Spirit realm. (2 hrs)

7. The Prayer Shawl and The Hebrew Alphabet
Richard shares on the Jewish Prayer Shawl while wearing one. A great healing message from Numbers to Revelation. A woman touched the hem of Jesus' garment and was healed. The 2nd message parallels the 22 Hebrew letters with the 22 mysteries in the New Testament. This is one of my most unique messages. (2 hrs)

8. Overcoming Giants / How to Receive Revelation Knowledge – Richard shares on the 5 giants King David killed, where they came from, and the meaning of their names. He also compares the lives of David, Jesus and the body of Christ and how we overcome the enemy. The 2nd hour includes how we can receive and retain revelation, wisdom, and knowledge. Richard shares how to hear from God for direction and instruction. (2 hrs)

$20.00 each or any three for $50.00
Bonus Buy - All 8 DVDs for
only $130.00
Includes 1st class postage

Call 205-622-5022 or mail check or money order to:

Operation Healing Ministries
Richard Madison
PO Box 205
Oakman, AL 35579

www.rickmadison.org - VISA-MC-AMEX & DISC.

Messages on CD & Cassette

1. Walking Miracle Testimony
2. Receiving the Holy Ghost
3. The Names of God
4. Purposes of the Holy Ghost
5. Gifts of the Holy Spirit
6. Are You In The Fire?
7. What God is Doing Now
8. Daniel's 70th Week
9. The Glory of God
10. The Bible Code
11. Visions and Dreams
12. Healings and Miracles
13. Encounters of the 3rd Kind
14. Eagle Christians
15. The Name of Jesus
16. Enoch and Elijah
17. Arise & Shine
18. Waiting on God
19. Overcoming Giants
20. Satan's 3 Missing Stones
21. Why Jesus Died on a Cross
22. Deserts & Caves
23. Hebrew Alphabet I
24. Hebrew Alphabet II
25. Mystery of the Hours
26. Give the Woman What She Wants
27. What The Fig Tree Represents
28. Miracles I Have Seen
29. Mephibosheth & Jabez
30. What is Pentecost?
31. Jesus, the Messiah
32. Issues, Infirmities & Inabilities
33. We Must Die to Live
34. The Salt Covenant
35. The Lion, Bear and the Serpent
36. Eight Raptures – Enoch to the White Throne Judgment
37. Ashes of the Red Heifer
38. The Millennial Reign
39. Signs of Jesus' Return
40. God Warns His People 1st
41. The Prophecy of Jesus
42. God's Will for You
43. Revelation Knowledge
44. The Blood of Jesus
45. The Word of God
46. Hidden Manna
47. Job and King Tut
48. A Still Small Voice
49. Power Comes After Prayer
50. The Five-Fold Ministry
51. Are You a Believer?
52. The Anointed Ones
53. The Peace of God
54. The Two Witnesses
55. World Events & US Presidents
56. The Rapture
57. Entertaining Angels
58. 7 Feasts of Israel
59. The Prayer Shawl
60. Wonders and Signs
61. All of Our Weapons
62. Days of Creation
63. Needs Met in the Glory
64. Intercessory Prayer
65. The Atonement
66. Walking by Faith
67. Satan, UFO's & Deception
68. Seeing in the Spirit

Order online at www. rickmadison..org
All tapes or CD's are $8.00 each
Includes 1ST class postage

About the Author

Richard Madison is an ordained International Evangelist. He and his wife Paula minister full time. Richard has a powerful healing and prophetic ministry with a unique sense of humor. Richard conducts camp meetings, rallies, conventions and revivals in all types of churches. His ministry began in 1986 after waking up out of a 27 day coma and walking out of a wheelchair. He has ministered out of the U.S. 34 times in 10 countries. During an extended fast, God taught Richard about the anointing, the gifts of the Spirit, and how to hear the voice of God. Richard has seen many miracles such as blind eyes opened, deaf ears unstopped and 20 people awakened out of comas. Richard's depth of the Word has captivated and instructed thousands since 1986. Richard has appeared on It's Supernatural with Sid Roth, Celebration with Marcus and Joni Lamb, and The 700 Club with Pat Robertson. Richard's own TV ministry is on Christian Television Network (**CTN**) on Dish Network ch. 267, Direct TV ch. 376, Glory Star ch. 117, and Sky Angel ch. 136. Sunday at 8 pm CT / Tuesday at 10:30 pm CT.

Please contact him at:
Operation Healing Ministries
PO Box 205 • Oakman, AL 35579 • (205) 622 - 5022
www.rickmadison.org
Email - rick@rickmadison.com

BOOK ORDER FORM		
Qty	Price	Total
BOOK - Raised from the Dead		
	$15.00	
BOOK - Levantado De La Muerte		
	$15.00	
BOOK - The Anointing, Power, & Gifts of God		
	$15.00	
BOOK – End Time Prophecy Revealed		
	$15.00	
BOOK – God's Strategy for Tragedy by Ben Godwin		
	$15.00	
BONUS BUY – Any Three Books*		
	$40.00	
BONUS BUY – Any Three Books & Any Three DVDs*		
	$75.00	
BONUS BUY – Case of Any 40 Books*		
	$300.00	
GRAND TOTAL (Free Shipping for continental US Orders)		

*Note :Please indicate which Books and/or DVDs you desire.

DVD ORDER FORM		
Qty	Price	Total
End Time Prophecies Volume 1		
	$20.00	
End Time Prophecies Volume 2		
	$20.00	
Miracle Testimony / Ashes of the Red Heifer		
	$20.00	
Interview with Sid Roth / Anointing & Funny Stories		
	$20.00	
Faith Series		
	$20.00	
Entertaining Angels & Seeing in the Spirit		
	$20.00	
The Prayer Shawl & The Hebrew Alphabet		
	$20.00	
Overcoming Giants & Receiving Revelation Knowledge		
	$20.00	
BONUS BUY – Pick Any Three DVDs*		
	$50.00	
BONUS BUY – All 8 DVDs		
	$130.00	
GRAND TOTAL (Free Shipping for continental US Orders)		

*Note :Please indicate which DVDs you desire.

Qty	Sermon	Total
	SERMON ORDER FORM (All Sermons are $8 each)*	
GRAND TOTAL (Free Shipping for continental US Orders)		

*Note :Please indicate if you desire a cassette tape rather than a CD of any of these sermons.